VSTO 3.0 for Office 2007 Programming

Get to grips with programming Office 2007 using
Visual Studio Tools for Office

Vivek Thangaswamy

PUBLISHING

BIRMINGHAM - MUMBAI

VSTO 3.0 for Office 2007 Programming

Copyright © 2009 Packt Publishing

First published: March 2009

Production Reference: 1040309

Published by Packt Publishing Ltd.
32 Lincoln Road
Olton
Birmingham, B27 6PA, UK.

ISBN 978-1-847197-52-8

www.packtpub.com

Cover Image by Parag Kadam (paragvkadam@gmail.com)

Credits

Author

Vivek Thangaswamy

Reviewers

Helmut Obertanner

Maarten van Stam

N Satheesh Kumar

Senior Acquisition Editor

Douglas Paterson

Development Editor

Dilip Venkatesh

Technical Editor

Rakesh Shejwal

Copy Editor

Sumathi Sridhar

Indexer

Monica Ajmera

Production Editorial Manager

Abhijeet Deobhakta

Editorial Team Leader

Akshara Aware

Project Team Leader

Lata Basantani

Project Coordinator

Joel Goveya

Proofreader

Dirk Manuel

Production Coordinator

Shantanu Zagde

Cover Work

Shantanu Zagde

About the Author

Vivek Thangaswamy is a software solutions developer and technical writer, living and working in the enjoyable surroundings of Chennai city in India. Although his range of technical competence stretches across various platforms and lines of businesses, his specialization is in the area of Microsoft enterprise application architectures and Microsoft server based product integration. Vivek is working with Microsoft technologies such as .NET, SharePoint, BizTalk, VSTO, and MS Performance Point Server for one of the world's largest Software Services companies. He holds several Microsoft certifications and Microsoft MVP awards. He holds a bachelors degree in Information Technology, and is currently pursuing his Masters in Business Administration (Finance). Vivek loves to spend time with his friends, and writing poems in his mother tongue.

To my brother, Arun Thangaswamy, who shaped me for the future and always brings out the best in me.

To my mother and father, who taught me to think, and gave me the courage to dream bigger.

To all of my friends, who bring joy to my life.

About the Reviewers

Helmut Obertanner was born in 1968 in Munich, Germany. After school, he became an Electronic Engineer, and his first experience with building computers came in 1985. On graduation, he started repairing Commodore Business Machines (PET). Later on, he specialized in repairing the legendary C64, Amiga and Atari consoles, and the very first PCs. From 1990 to 1995, he worked as a systems engineer, building heterogeneous networks with Windows NT, Novell, and Apple. After that, he was administrator for an architecture company, responsible for the entire IT communications, CAD, and Office support. In 2000, he changed to being an IT systems supplier, and worked as a technical consultant for Exchange Server, Antivirus, Firewalls, and Backup/Restore solutions. In 2002, he started developing Software, building Outlook add-ins with VB6. When the Microsoft .NET Framework 1.0 came out, he was one of the first to try and build managed add-ins for Office. Due to his technical knowledge, sample codes, and help to other Office Developers he was awarded the MVP for VSTO by Microsoft. He is always interested in working on new technologies.

Currently, he is working for PHARMATECHNIK GmbH & Co. KG in Starnberg, Germany, building software for pharmacies using .NET and C#.

Maarten van Stam holds a B.Sc in Computer science (Graduation in 1996, HIO, The Hague, The Netherlands), and has worked as a software engineer for over 20 years. He started programming dBase and Clipper (DOS) systems in the early 80's, followed by Pascal and C++ in the late 80's, C++ and VB "for Windows" in the early 90's, and continues to program in VB.NET and C# as part of the Microsoft's .NET Framework.

Maarten has specialized in Office development, .NET, and VSTO, and has received the Microsoft MVP award in the area of Visual Developer-VSTO for voluntarily sharing expertise with others. In addition to this role, Maarten takes part in several TAP programs, beta tests, software design reviews and advisory councils for software tools such as Visual Studio Team System and Microsoft Office. In addition to working in the software business professionally, Maarten is also an organizational member in the "Software Development Network", currently the largest developer community group in the Netherlands (www.sdn.nl).

Besides tech-reading *Beginning Office 2007 Development with VSTO,* Maarten also reviewed *Visual Studio Tools for Office 2007: VSTO for Excel, Word, and Outlook* by Eric Carter and Eric Lippert (ISBN 0321533216).

Maarten's insights can be read and followed on www.maartenvanstam.nl, where you can find his blog all aspects of software development.

N Satheesh Kumar has a Bachelor's Degree in Computer Science Engineering and has around 12 years of experience in software development life cycle, project and program management. He is also a PMI-certified Project Management Professional (PMP). He started his career developing software applications using Borland software products in a company based in India, and then moved to the United Arab Emirates and continued developing applications using Borland Delphi and customizing Great Plain Dynamics (now known as Microsoft Dynamics) for an automobile company. Later, he spent three years designing and developing application software using Microsoft products for a top multinational company, and then spent a couple of years in project management and program management activities. Currently, he works as a technical architect for a top retail company based in the United States. He works with the latest Microsoft technologies and has published many articles on LINQ and other features of .NET.

Satheesh is the author of the book *LINQ Quickly,* and has co-authored the book *Software Testing with Visual Studio Team System 2008.*

I would like to thank my family members and friends for their continued support in my career and success.

Table of Contents

Preface

Welcome to *VSTO 3.0 for Office 2007 Programming*. This book covers Visual Studio Tools for Office programming, with a primary emphasis on the several new VSTO programming features available for Microsoft Office 2007. VSTO is a phenomenon that means different things to different people. This book introduces developers to VSTO as a platform for developing enterprise solutions based on Microsoft Office application.

This book covers Microsoft VSTO objects for Microsoft Office applications such as Word, Excel, PowerPoint, Visio, Outlook, and Project, which can be a significant challenge for the typical VBA developer—one set of target readers for this book. This book is focused more on the features of VSTO and how to work with the heavily-built Office object models. Although you might not be familiar with .NET programming, this book will help you to adapt easily to the new VSTO with .NET programming environment.

VSTO brings the Office applications to the .NET programming world. With VSTO 3.0, you can create add-ins for the six Microsoft Office applications, customize the Ribbon feature of the Microsoft Office 2007 suite, and create application-level custom task panes. This book strives to follow the same model. It explains VSTO's concepts and basic programming in a way that helps beginners to get started and helps advanced users to get better. In addition to this, the book includes chapters for all of the Office applications, which describe how the programming and customization works, what its requirements are, and how it will simplify typical tasks.

What this book covers

Chapter 1 provides a panoramic overview of Visual Studio Tools for Office. This chapter provides you with a firm grounding in what VSTO really is. We look at how VSTO addresses the Microsoft Office 2007 customization area, its feature set, and its architecture.

Chapter 2 starts by explaining the object model and programming approach in InfoPath 2007. We then take a look at how we can customize InfoPath with Visual Studio 2008. The later part of the chapter explains how to work on task pane creation, development of add-ins, and so on.

Chapter 3 begins with a description of creating a Word solution using Visual Studio 2008, and as we move further, the chapter explains how to create document-level solutions and application-level solutions. It then explains the deployment process. It also covers key Word objects, with examples of how to work with SQL data manipulation, and so on.

Chapter 4 takes a look at working with Excel objects, and covers key objects with example solutions. It focuses on explaining host items and host controls and provides examples of some common solutions. It also gives you an idea of worksheet protection, smart tags, charts, and so on, with the help of examples.

Chapter 5 starts the chapter with an overview of Outlook objects and moves on to Outlook folder manipulation, mail item processing and working with meetings and appointments. In the later part of the chapter, we work with Ribbon customization for Outlook, with examples and many such customizations for Outlook.

Chapter 6 covers three Office applications: PowerPoint, Visio, and Project. Here, we work with shapes in Visio, Ribbon customization for PowerPoint, and dynamic project item manipulation, and so on.

Who this book is for

This book is aimed at .NET developers who are familiar with C# and who want to get to grips with programming Office 2007. The book will also be useful for people who already have experience with VBA and programming Office, but are ready to take the next step into the more powerful world of Office programming with VSTO.

Conventions

In this book, you will find a number of styles of text that distinguish between different kinds of information. Here are some examples of these styles, and an explanation of their meaning.

Code words in text are shown as follows: "Zack used the `AfterNewPresentation` event and developed a solution for it".

A block of code will be set as follows:

```
private void ThisAddIn_Startup(object sender, System.EventArgs e)
{
    // Creating PowerPoint presentation with single slide in it
    // Using the PowerPoint object instance adding the
    // Slide with text title structure to the current Presentation
        PowerPoint.Presentation PacktPresentation = this.Application.
            Presentations.Add(Microsoft.Office.Core.MsoTriState.
            msoTriStateMixed);
}
```

New terms and **important words** are introduced in a bold-type font. Words that you see on the screen, in menus or dialog boxes for example, appear in our text like this: "As it can be seen in the following screenshot, **Say Hello World** is displayed in a message box:".

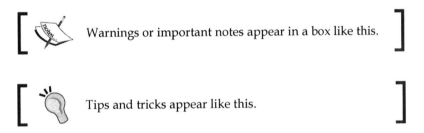

Warnings or important notes appear in a box like this.

Tips and tricks appear like this.

Reader feedback

Feedback from our readers is always welcome. Let us know what you think about this book—what you liked or may have disliked. Reader feedback is important for us to develop titles that you really get the most out of.

To send us general feedback, simply send an email to feedback@packtpub.com, making sure that you mention the book title in the subject of your message.

If there is a book that you need and would like to see us publish, please send us a note via the **SUGGEST A TITLE** form on www.packtpub.com, or send an email to suggest@packtpub.com.

If there is a topic that you have expertise in and you are interested in either writing or contributing to a book on, see our author guide on www.packtpub.com/authors.

Customer support

Now that you are the proud owner of a Packt book, we have a number of things to help you to get the most from your purchase.

Downloading the example code for the book

Visit `http://www.packtpub.com/files/code/7528_Code.zip` to directly download the example code.

Errata

Although we have taken every care to ensure the accuracy of our contents, mistakes do happen. If you find a mistake in one of our books—maybe a mistake in text or code—we would be grateful if you would report this to us. By doing this you can save other readers from frustration, and help to improve subsequent versions of this book. If you find any errata, report them by visiting `http://www.packtpub.com/support`, selecting your book, clicking on the **let us know** link, and entering the details of your errata. Once your errata are verified, your submission will be accepted and the errata added to any list of existing errata. Any existing errata can be viewed by selecting your title from `http://www.packtpub.com/support`.

Piracy

Piracy of copyright material on the Internet is an ongoing problem across all media. At Packt, we take the protection of our copyright and licenses very seriously. If you come across any illegal copies of our works in any form on the Internet, please provide the location address or website name immediately, so that we can pursue a remedy.

Please contact us at `copyright@packtpub.com` with a link to the suspected pirated material.

We appreciate your help in protecting our authors, and our ability to bring you valuable content.

Questions

You can contact us at `questions@packtpub.com` if you are having a problem with any aspect of this book, and we will do our best to address it.

1
Visual Studio Tools for Office (VSTO)

VSTO is a framework for the development of solutions for Microsoft Office tools. By using VSTO and what is known as managed code, developers can build Office solutions. Before we begin the chapter, let us see an overview of what we are going to cover in this chapter. This book is for Office Developers using Visual Studio Tools for Office. This chapter will make you comfortable with Visual Studio Tools for Office 3.0. We will be covering:

- What is Microsoft VSTO?
- Why do we need VSTO 3.0?
- New features added in VSTO 3.0 as compared with the older version
- The architecture of VSTO and the tools' approaches
- Infrastructural setup—system requirements, installation, and so on
- How VSTO is integrated with Visual Studio 2008, and its integrated design and debugging features
- New features in the next version of VSTO, and how VSTO can be further improved

VSTO helps you to build document-level solutions, where a solution is specific to the document for which it is deployed. You can build application-level solutions by using the application-level **add-in** for your solution development. The application-level add-in is accessible to all of the documents processed through that particular application.

What is Microsoft VSTO?

VSTO is a platform for Microsoft Office solution development, built on top of .NET framework. The latest release is version 3.0. Starting with VSTO 3.0, developers have integrated Office clients into the Visual Studio designer and the .NET layers on top of the native object models.

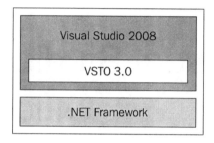

The image above represents how VSTO has been integrated with the Visual Studio 2008 environment. Now, the term "Office solutions" appears a lot. You may have questions like—"What exactly, is an Office solution anyway? What kind of Office solutions can be developed using VSTO?". Let's answer these questions.

An **Office solution** is a solution developed for Microsoft Office applications, including Word, Excel, InfoPath, Access, or PowerPoint. With the help of VSTO, developers can build Office solutions using what is known as **managed code**.

Managed code is program code that executes under the supervision of a .NET Framework Common Language Runtime. Programs in any programming language can be compiled using either managed or unmanaged code. Code that is built on the .NET framework is meant to be managed code. Managed code brings easy deployment to your VSTO solution, as compared to **VBA (Visual Basic for Applications)**. VBA is a programming combination of Visual Basic associated with an integrated development environment for Microsoft Office applications.

Unlike VSTO, VBA doesn't support programming languages. VSTO gives you the full support of a programming language to build Microsoft Office solutions. VSTO helps you to build a secure and safe solution for your Office application. All of the VBA scripts will be stored inside the document for which you are programming, while VSTO brings you the new concept called document-level solutions and application-level solutions.

Using VSTO, Office developers can build solutions such as Add-Ins; Add-Ins are additional program components that can be added to Office applications by using VSTO. For example, Microsoft offers a few free add-ins for Office 2007 licensed users, such as the 2007 Microsoft Office add-in **Microsoft Save as PDF or XPS** — this add-in facilitates the saving of a document in PDF or XPS format. You can also customize existing Office application features, and you can program against existing options available in the Office application. Let's say you need to save or export all of the content from Microsoft Office Word 2007 to Microsoft Office Excel 2007 on the click event of a button placed on the toolbar, or during some action. You can create an add-in for this kind of activity using VSTO. This is one scenario where you can use a VSTO add-in for your Office solution development.

Before VSTO, Office developers had to use VBA, VB6, or C++ to create so called shared COM Add-Ins. All Add-Ins share the same address space, and if one fails, the host application or all other Add-Ins crash. Unlike VSTO, VBA code is written directly in the Office application's IDE and is compiled at run-time. All VBA scripts are stored inside the document for which you were programming. In VSTO, this is termed a **document-level solution**, where the solution is specific to the document for which it is deployed. Similarly, in VSTO, document level add-ins are delivered within a specific document. For example, let's say that you include functions in a specific Microsoft Office Word document — the functions are available only when you open that particular Word document. Document level add-ins are relevant only to Word and Excel. **Document-level customizations** are the VSTO version of VBA macros in Word or Excel.

VSTO introduces a new concept called **application-level solutions**. With an application-level solution, the solution is accessible for all documents processed through that particular application. You can build application-level solutions by using the application-level add-in for your solution development.

VSTO gives you two fully-supported programming languages in which to build Microsoft Office solutions that will run in all Microsoft Office applications — C#, VB.NET, or XML. As a VSTO programmer, you will need to have a basic knowledge of C# to program Office applications using C#. In this book, we will assume that you have a basic knowledge of C# concepts such as classes, namespaces, and methods. In addition, you should know the basics of XML.

The following MSDN reference link will help you learn about .NET and C#: `http://msdn.microsoft.com/en-us/vcsharp/aa336804.aspx`

In most of the Office 2007 applications, Microsoft has used **XML (Extensible Markup Language)** as the standard format for data and UI processing. For example, InfoPath forms save data in XML format. C# brings you great programming support for XML and Office applications. Office already has built-in support for an XML-based customization model, of which VSTO takes full advantage. Using C# classes and simple XML, VSTO simplifies the connection between .NET, and the server and Office systems.

- VSTO leverages two powerful technologies that you may be familiar with—C# and XML. C# is one of the most powerful programming languages supported by Microsoft .NET frameworks.

- VSTO gives full flexibility to programs using C# and VB.NET programming language for Office 2007 applications.

- You, as a VSTO programmer, need to have a basic knowledge of C#, in order to program Office applications using C#.

So, for instance, instead of having a Word macro that you need to run in order to create the document you want, you could simply transfer the information to a Word template and have Office create the document for you! VSTO thus provides data-caching capabilities.

Why VSTO 3.0?

VSTO is a simple, but powerful framework for Office solution development. The framework brings an amazing number of benefits to the hands of every Office developer—form controls, classes, granular security, server scalability, object-oriented features, integrity, easy deployment, and many others.

Safer managed code extensions

VSTO allows managed and unmanaged code to be seamlessly put together into the same .NET assembly. This allows the developers to retain unmanaged code that cannot be ported over to the .NET framework without completely re-writing it. The Microsoft Office document or workbook with a linked or referenced managed code assembly is said to have managed code extensions. Managed extensions can be created by using VSTO on Microsoft Excel or Word, which are similar to macros but are much safer. With VSTO, you can create a template that only needs to be loaded with data.

Data caching

Data caching, simply put, is storing data in memory for quick access. A Microsoft Office Word document or Excel workbook has a hidden control rooted inside it called the **Runtime Storage Control**, which stores cached data. VSTO provides data-caching capabilities as well as a `ServerDocument` class in C# that can be used by an application external to Office (for example, the Winform application) to manipulate the data cache without accessing the object model of Word or Excel.

Feature customization

VSTO 3.0 gives you great control in being able to customize Office applications with reusable classes. Unlike VBA developers, VSTO developers are not limited to the VBA function library. VSTO provides a wide variety of classes, objects, and events to build business solutions for Microsoft Office. Using VSTO, developers can customize features for Office applications. These can be as simple as a button on the application's Command bar or adding custom task panes, or as complex as a data report template with access to different data sources.

User Interface customization

VSTO provides Windows Forms controls that help you to develop a rich **User Interface (UI)** for your Office solution. By using a wide variety of control sets, VSTO developers can build rich data views for users. Each and every type of Windows Forms control has its own set of properties, methods, and events that make it suitable for different needs.

VSTO makes it easy to build rich User Interfaces by using controls inside the document and the Task Pane. For instance, you can create an animated one-button command to generate a form letter. For example, say a company has data content stored in its server, and a user wants to refer some content from the server while working in the document and without disturbing the current document view. Using VSTO, you can make the server content available inside the Task Pane of the document without interfering with the user's current work.

Smart tags

New for VSTO 3.0 and Office 2007, smart tags are strings that an Office application recognizes in a document. With Smart tags enabled, Microsoft Office Word attempts to recognize certain types of data in a document, visually indicated by a purple, dotted underline. Clicking on a smart tag brings up a list of possible actions for that particular data type. VSTO provides object models to Office developers, which can be used to create smart tags for documents and workbooks.

WPF support

Windows Presentation Foundation (WPF) controls is a technology product of Microsoft Corporation. WPF can be used to build a rich and attractive look and feel for the user. WPF can be used in VSTO development environment, which supports C# programming, whereas VBA lacks this support. VSTO's visual designer supports the use of Windows Forms and Windows Presentation Foundation controls. WPF provides a reliable programming model for building client-based and web-based applications, and presents a clear separation between the business logic and the UI.

Visual designers

VSTO provides visual designers for Office applications such as Word 2007, Excel 2007, and others that appear inside the Visual Studio **IDE (Integrated Development Environment)**. Creating a form in the Visual Studio IDE is as easy as dragging and dropping the form into the Microsoft Office document. Developers gain access to many tools and features in Visual Studio's IDE, such as IntelliSense (Microsoft's implementation of auto completion in the Visual Studio IDE), drag and drop controls, and data sources. VSTO also provides the Ribbon Visual Designer that lets you customize the Office Ribbon and program it by using a simple .NET application-like programming model. The following image explains how IntelliSense helps developers using Visual Studio IDE.

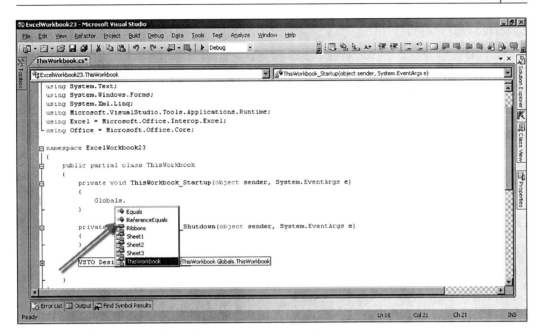

Security improvements

The VSTO security model involves wide support from Trust Center in Microsoft Office and the Visual Studio Tools for Office runtime, which helps resolve the security issues common to VBA code. There are many disadvantages to the VBA security model. An abundant number of viruses are easily developed using VBA macros. To run VBA macros safely, you have to set the security to high on the user machine, and digitally sign the code. More importantly, these operations need to be performed manually by the user. In VSTO 3.0, the Security Model has been changed. VSTO builds the security policy that is required to run and debug your solution on your computer every time that you build a project. The Assemblies are signed before publishing—this is done by Visual Studio 2008. Preferably, you obtain a certificate from a globally-acknowledged Certificate Authority or from an internal Certificate Authority, if the solution is only for an internal solution, and sign the manifests using the signing properties page in Visual Studio. Later, you publish the solution to its appropriate location.

Maintainability

VSTO solutions developed for an Office system are easier to maintain. Updating the deployed solutions, changing the code, and updating a single assembly will help more resources doing the same thing in multiple copies of the same documents. All of the code will reside inside the assembly—a partially-compiled code library that contains the logical unit of code inside it as a single dynamic link library (.dll) file. With macros, the script resided inside the Office documents. Whenever you wanted to update the code, you had to modify every single document that contained it. With VSTO 3.0, managing application-level add-ins can be done by simply changing the code and updating the single assembly, instead of doing the same thing for multiple copies of the same document.

What's new in VSTO 3.0?

VSTO 3.0 is loaded with a wide variety of new features, and reloaded with enhancements of some of the key existing features. VSTO 3.0's new features target Microsoft Office 2007 (Office 12) tools with new functionalities and enhanced existing features. Let's list some of the key new features that are available in VSTO 3.0 that improve Office solution development work:

- **Document-level customizations**: Document-level customizations are customized solutions that reside in a single document. Document-level customization using VSTO is one of the key features added in this new version of VSTO. VSTO supports document-level solutions for Microsoft Office Word, Microsoft Office Excel, and Microsoft Office InfoPath.

- **Application level add-ins**: Application level add-ins are created as a managed code assembly using VSTO that will be loaded when the relevant Microsoft Office application is launched. VSTO 3.0 provides access to .NET objects and controls that you can program directly.

- **Visual Designers for Ribbons**: Ribbons are the new way of organizing related commands. Visually, they appear as controls. Visual Designer provides advanced tools and supports developers in creating and designing custom Ribbons more easily.

- **Task Panes**: The Task Pane helps users to access information quickly and more conveniently. Task Panes can be shown or hidden in the Office application user interface depending on the user's preference.

- **Form regions**: Form regions are new ways to customize the user interface of the standard Microsoft Office Outlook 2007. For instance, VSTO 3.0 provides a Windows Forms-based design and development environment, in Visual Studio 2008. This allows Office developers to design and code the new Outlook form regions in single development environment and brings most of the Windows Forms to the hosting environment of Outlook.

- **Workflow support**: VSTO provides visual designer support for developers to create Workflows using Visual Studio 2008. A Wizard option is used to create Workflows and directly assign these to the deployment location.

- **SharePoint support**: New objects in VSTO help developers to program in Office applications for SharePoint. You can extend your Office client applications using VSTO and integrate them with a SharePoint Portal into an enterprise solution such as Customer Relationship Management, Supply Chain Management, and other similar applications.

- **Deployment using ClickOnce**: New for VSTO 3, ClickOnce deployment technology allows Windows-based applications to be deployed and run with minimal user interaction. The security zone will limit the permissions and actions for applications that are deployed using ClickOnce technology.

- **Word content controls**: Content controls are containers within which specific types of content, such as dates, lists, pictures, or text, can be placed.

- **Rich user interface controls**: Office solutions can be built with rich and easy-to-access user interfaces. For instance, you can create an actions pane with windows controls, which has data interaction with other data sources in the actions pane.

- **Support for other Office applications**: There is even a complex object model for Visio, which is somewhat different from the other Office applications, and can be challenging to understand. In Visio, each shape is represented as an object that you drag-and-drop onto the page from stencils. Understanding and manipulating these objects is the key to creating Visio applications solution.

 Stencils are collections of Visio shapes that you can add to your drawings, and that are contained in a Visio file.

VSTO architecture

Architecture is the essential association of a system that comes to life in its components, their associations to each other and to the environment, and the main beliefs guiding its design, and evolution. VSTO applications are composed of Office applications and .NET assemblies.

- **Office applications**: VSTO exposes objects that make it easier to program Office applications. These include objects that enhance the application and process the data that the application uses. One of the most important points to understand is that the Word and Excel editors provide a view of a Word or Excel document. Using these editors, you can edit and format the document as though you were working directly in an Office application.

- **.NET assemblies**: These contain **Intermediate Language** (IL) code. Metadata, which is binary information describing your program, is stored in memory and is part of a .NET assembly. In addition to metadata information, assemblies also have a special file called a **Manifest**. The Manifest contains information about the current version of the assembly.

The core components of VSTO Architecture are document-level customizations, application-level add-ins, and a Data Model at the document level. The new architecture of VSTO allows Office applications to be written and run with macros embedded inside the application.

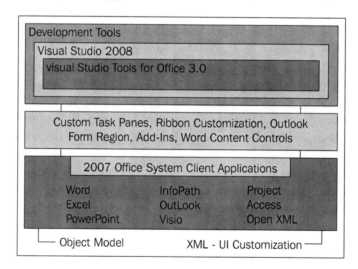

The preceding image represents the Microsoft Office 2007 Solution Logical Architecture. VSTO enables Office developers to build document-level customizations for InfoPath, Word, and Excel documents, whereas for Outlook, PowerPoint, and Visio, there are no document-level customization features supported by VSTO.

VSTO provides very good support for object-oriented programming, a feature lacking in VBA scripting. VSTO provides full support for the C# programming language, allowing the implementation of object-oriented programming in Office solutions. Object-oriented programming is a kind of programming that relates coding blocks to objects. In other words, object-oriented programming is a software programming approach in which the structures of a program are based on objects' interaction with other objects, in order to perform or execute tasks.VSTO has several objects to work with in order to create applications using VSTO 3.0.

The architectural design of VSTO helps the Office developer in programming separately for application and data. The VSTO architecture design provides enhanced support for developing application-level solutions, and it exposes various objects that will make it easier for Office developers to program for Office applications. The most important point that you have to understand is that Word and Excel are the editors for the data they represent. Using these editors, you can edit and format the visually-displayed data. VSTO exposes a wide range of objects for enhancing the application and for processing the data inside the application for all of the Office applications that support it. Developing application level and document-level solutions is another architectural advancement in VSTO.

Development approaches

The types of solutions that we can create by using VSTO 3.0 fall into two categories, which we will use throughout this book — document-level solutions, and application-level solutions. Let's discuss each briefly.

Document-oriented approach

The document-oriented approach is designed specifically to get to the core of a Word or Excel document and include information that the document wasn't originally designed to support. VSTO 3.0 supports the creation of document-oriented approaches for InfoPath, Word, and Excel. Essentially, document-oriented approaches provide a document pointing to very specific tasks. An example of a document-oriented approach would be where uniform template kind of documents are managed inside a team or company without affecting the application of the document that they reside in.

A point to note is that the document-oriented approach will apply to most, but not all, Office 2007 applications.

Application-oriented approach

VSTO 3.0 is capable of creating application-oriented approaches for all of the applications in the Office 2007 suite. You can create and implement add-ins that add a wide range of functionalities and features to your Office application. The application-oriented approach replaces VBA, and adds new features such as add-ins for 2007 Microsoft Office applications that support enterprise solution development using VSTO. Furthermore, the approach supports the six applications in the 2007 Microsoft Office system, along with the tools and enhanced **application programming interfaces** (**APIs**) for customizing the Ribbon UI and creating custom task panes and add-ins. An API is a set of declarations of the functions or procedures provided in order to support requests made by computer programs.

VSTO development and deployment

The VSTO system 3.0 Runtime, which is the primary requirement to run the Office 2007 solutions, is built on VSTO. More importantly, the VSTO 3.0 is built into the Visual Studio 2008 installer. Service pack 1 for Visual Studio 2008 is available for users, which will improve the Visual Studio performance, and fix unknown bugs. The following VSTO related bug that used to load VSTO-derived Outlook Addins, was also fixed in Service Pack 1 — AddinLoader.DLL, is not signed. This DLL **MUST** be signed so as to enable Outlook to load any add-in developed under VSTO 2005, when user sets Macro security to **High**, and **Trust installed addins...** is **NOT** selected.

Creating Office applications through VSTO

VSTO is included in the Visual Studio 2008 release, which is a set of related libraries and designers for developing applications, along with add-ins for Microsoft Office 2003 and 2007. Microsoft has bundled VSTO 3.0 with Visual Studio 2008 for the first time, which also represents a considerable step forward in the development environment. Previously, developers had to install Visual Studio and VSTO separately in order to build a development environment. Also, it was necessary to perform manual configuration in order to enable debugging for Office solutions.

Microsoft Office remains the best Office application when it comes to automating processes, as well as for using different types of data sources for presenting data to the user. In VSTO 3.0, Microsoft Office tools have become more powerful for presenting data from business applications because Microsoft has made the Office development environment more developer-friendly by creating a new development environment that helps developers to build solutions that function inside Office applications. Thus, Microsoft Office developers are able to easily create solutions that can do more for their business, while reducing costs by reusing existing functionality available in the Office applications.

VSTO can even integrate with your existing ERP system, and increase your enterprise's growth. One leading logistics company has integrated its existing enterprise application with Microsoft Office application using Visual Studio Tools for Office. You can extend your Office client applications by using VSTO and integrate VSTO with the SharePoint Portal to provide enterprise solutions such as Office Business Applications, including Customer Relationship Management, Supply Chain Management, and many others.

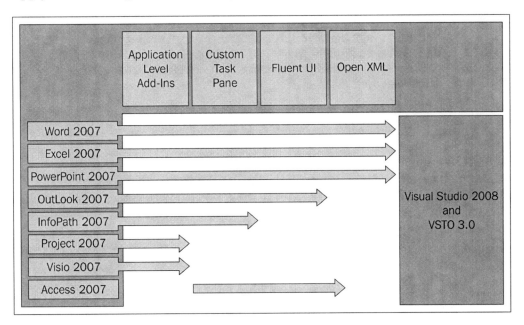

The preceding image represents Office 2007 and its extensibility using VSTO 3.0. All of the extensible features of VSTO 3.0 are not common to all of the Office 2007 applications. For example, application-level add-ins are not supported by Access 2007, and custom task panes are not supported by Visio 2007. VSTO documents contain a deployment manifest. The deployment manifest is an XML file that contains a description of the ClickOnce deployment, including the identification of and other information about the current ClickOnce application version that is to be deployed. The location of the VSTO document assembly will be available inside the document's deployment manifest. You can programmatically manipulate the deployment manifest of a document.

VSTO development environment

VSTO 3.0 is not a separate installation package for Visual Studio 2008. VSTO 3.0 reduces the development installation effort for Office developers. While installing Visual Studio 2008, VSTO 3.0 is installed along with the other frameworks and needed components.

You must install the Microsoft .NET Framework 3.5 redistributable package before installing the VSTO 3.0 Runtime. Developing and running Office customizations built with VSTO 3.0 requires the latest version of Microsoft Office 2007.

Package

The VSTO Runtime is installed when installing the Microsoft VSTO 3.0 redistributable package, which is essential for developing and deploying Office solutions using VSTO 3.0. A VSTO 3.0 redistributable package is the framework that brings the power and productivity of Visual Studio 2008 and the .NET framework to business solutions built on the Microsoft Office 2007 application.

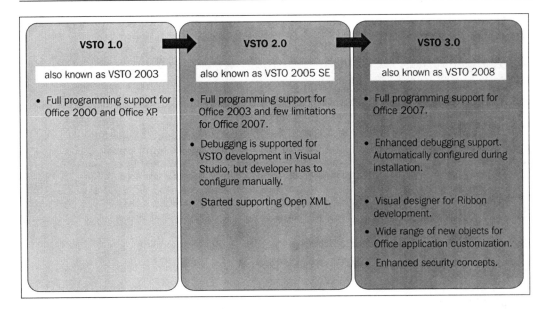

The preceding image explains the version history of VSTO, highlighting some of the key differences between the versions. The current release of VSTO supports only the programming languages VB.NET and C#. We can expect other programming languages support in the next version of VSTO.

Visual Studio integration

VSTO 3.0 provides a visual representation of Office applications inside the Visual Studio, in order to easily create a customized user interface. VSTO 3.0 is well integrated with Visual Studio 2008, which provides the integrity for Office developers to develop and deploy Microsoft Office solutions for Microsoft Office tools. Visual Studio 2008 enables developers to build scalable Office business applications, influence key Office UI features, support workflow, and create easier deployments. Office development is a part of Visual Studio 2008 Professional and later versions, which focuses mainly on the developers' compatibility and maintainability assurances.

Let's take a look at a typical VSTO project template for an Office 2007 application in Visual Studio 2008.

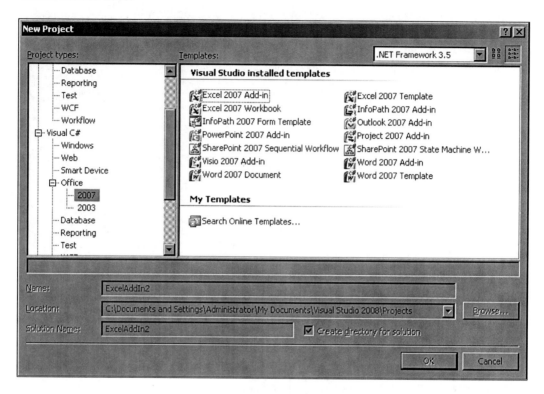

In the preceding image, you can see the VSTO project templates for Office 2007 applications in Visual Studio 2008. Visual Studio 2008 has been packed with all of the VSTO 3.0 components needed to build an Office solution using VSTO. When installing Visual Studio 2008, all of the related installations, including project templates for VSTO 3.0, Office development references, and others, have been installed and fully-integrated into the new Visual Studio 2008 development environment.

Creating VSTO solutions

Visual Studio 2008 is very fast, collaborative, and flexible in developing and delivering a wave of innovative new Microsoft technologies, including enhanced language and data features. C# and VB.NET programming supported in Office 2007 is one of the enhanced language features, and easy data interaction with other data sources, such as Microsoft SQL server, is one of the data features. These features ensure that developers can rapidly create connected applications, deliver next generation software practices, and overcome application software development challenges.

The preceding image represents the development environment of the Office solution. In this figure, the client represents the development environment machine; the VSTO 3.0 inside Visual Studio 2008 represents the VSTO integrated Visual Studio; Office 2007 Client tools are the Office applications, including Word, Excel, InfoPath, and others, that should be installed in the client machine for development.

The development environment using Visual Studio 2008 is capable of creating application-level, data-centric solutions with VSTO 3.0. The data-centric solutions are the functionalities that are siginificantly focused on data manipulation and data storage.

The Visual Studio 2008 development environment makes it possible to develop solutions with great design-time and runtime support for key Office 2007 System features, such as the Ribbon, Custom Task Panes, document-level solutions, Outlook forms regions, and so on.

The Ribbon is a new way of representing menu items in the Office application. In the new development environment, you have a visual designer within which you can drag-and-drop controls inside the Ribbon, and design your custom Ribbon menus easily. Even for a data-related operation such as creating data connections, you have a data connection wizard for easy creation of a data connection.

Let's take a look at how the Office project solution looks, once it's been created in Visual Studio 2008. For example, we'll load a Word 2007 document solution created with Visual Studio 2008 and VSTO, using project templates available in the development environment:

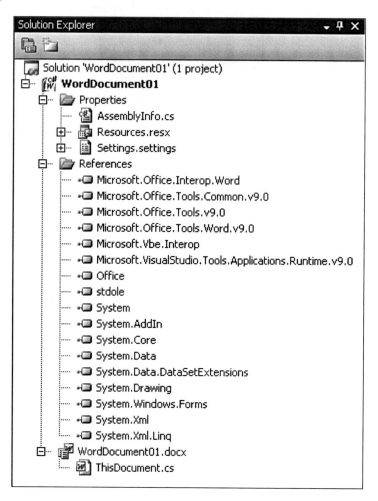

The preceding image represents how the Office project solution for Word 2007 has been created in Visual Studio 2008. You can see all of the references listed as **System. AddIn, System.Core**, and so on. These are loaded automatically as a part of the project template. This provides the developer with easy-to-start programming by eliminating the manual process of adding references and validating the solution.

Office developers can integrate business data into documents by using XML-based data/view separation and programmability. For example, in InfoPath, you can easily integrate business data with the InfoPath forms, and you can program the data of the InfoPath, storing it as a separate file in XML format. You can also present the data in different views, depending on how the user wants to see it, in the user interface. You can develop solutions using the combined Outlook object model.

Viewing IDE Windows

Visual Studio is a fabulous Microsoft product designed especially for development activities. It is one of the most widely-used development tools among developers across the globe. It is built on an IDE, and enables developers to build different types of applications using Microsoft technologies. IDE is a software application for developing new software programs and applications that provides broad facilities to programmers for software development.

In general, IDE consists of a source code editor, compilers, and debuggers. Most readers will be familiar with the Visual Studio IDE. Visual Studio 2008 has an appearance similar to previous IDEs, but with more enhancements. By default, Microsoft Visual Studio IDE will provide you with IntelliSense, debugging, compilers for .NET programming, access to control controls, and the ability to build solutions. The latest enhancements such as visual designer for Ribbon, drag-and-drop controls, and enhanced debugging for Office applications will reduce the development time and increase the productivity of developers.

The in-built VSTO object model is designed to support .NET. And it's also simple! Many common functions are packaged and well-integrated. In the new version, tools such as Word, Excel, and InfoPath's target windows, are integrated directly into the IDE interface. This helps Office developers to build solutions without needing an advanced knowledge of the underlying object model. VSTO also has visual designers for Word 2007 and Excel 2007 that are in the Visual Studio IDE.

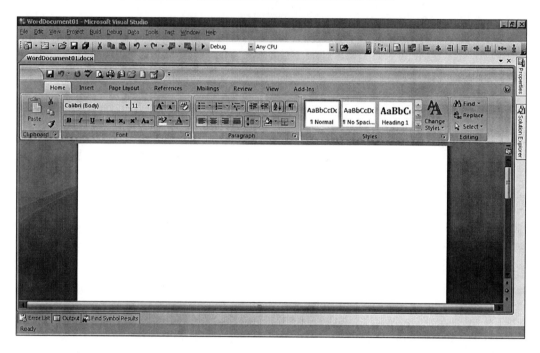

In the preceding image, we can see how the visual designer for Word 2007 appears in Visual Studio 2008. In this environment, you have the drag-and-drop functionality and other easy-to-design layouts for the use of an Office developer. Visual Studio 2008 brings the visual designer for other Office tools such as Excel and Infopath into the IDE. In a similar way, the Visual Studio 2008 IDE brings the visual Ribbon designer for Office tools into the interface. The Ribbon designer allows an Office developer to visually design an Office Ribbon (officially called the Office Fluent user interface) using the well-known drag-and-drop interface, and interact with the Ribbon using standard .NET code.

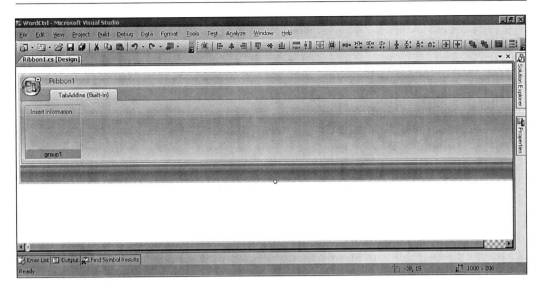

The preceding image shows the visual designer for the Ribbon in Office solution development, which simplifies the Ribbon development process for Office developers by providing drag-and-drop controls and easy access to resources. Similarly, Visual Studio 2008 simplifies and speeds up the development process of the actions pane, document-specific Task Panes, creating application-specific custom Task Panes, and Outlook Form Region Designer.

Debugging

Debugging is one of the most important tasks in software development, and a task that all developers will have run into many times in their programming lives. Developers have several debugging alternatives available for debugging their .NET applications that have DLL files in the Visual Studio IDE.

Visual Studio 2008 provides a strong set of build and debugging tools for Office solution development using VSTO 3.0. This is a big improvement over VSTO 2.0, which did not provide preconfigured debugging options. During configuration of the build, developers can select the components that they want to build, and exclude those that they want to avoid for the current build. A developer has the flexibility to build configurations for solutions as well as projects.

What can we expect in the next version?

The following points list some of the features we can expect in the next version of VSTO, based on the author's analysis and experiences as a VSTO developer:

- Presently, VSTO 3.0 supports VB.NET and C# for Office solution development. In future releases of VSTO, we can expect support for other languages such as C++, which will help C++ developers to build VSTO solutions.

- VSTO 3.0 smart tags are limited to document-level solutions in Office applications. They cannot be used in application-level solutions. Therefore we can expect Microsoft to add this feature in a future version of VSTO.

- Building workflow activities inside of Office applications by using VSTO and a Visual Studio environment is another feature that we can expect in the next release. Interoperability of data and applications is at the core of windows workflow, and progress in VSTO helps us to reorganize workflow-oriented development.

- Using VSTO to create document-level custom Tasks Panes for Visio applications should also be added in a future version. This will be useful for managing custom shapes for Visio users.

Summary

Microsoft has rebuilt the Office development framework, VSTO, with a wide variety of features, and has also enhanced most of the existing features. In this chapter, we went through the features and functionalities of VSTO 3.0. You have seen what VSTO is about and how it can be used for Office 2007 application customization. You have learned how VSTO is integrated with Visual Studio 2008, and how easy it is for a developer to create a solution using Visual Studio 2008. You have also seen some of its key features such as custom Task panes, Ribbons, Add-ins and document-level customization, and so on, and how these are helpful for Office developers. In this chapter you have also seen the architecture of VSTO and IDE for VSTO development, and have learned the enhanced debugging features for VSTO in Visual Studio IDE. You have learned the concept of object-oriented support in VSTO Office solution development, and have also seen the C# programming language and .NET framework technology platform support for Office development.

2
Microsoft Office InfoPath Programming

Microsoft Office InfoPath, as the name suggests, is a part of the Microsoft Office Tool suite. InfoPath aids programmers, as well as Microsoft Office users. Programmers can use InfoPath to design XML-based forms, and users of Office applications can open these forms and easily enter data into them. Microsoft Office InfoPath was first released as a part of Microsoft Office 2003, but has been considerably enhanced since then.

In this chapter, we'll discuss the following:

- InfoPath 2007 in Visual Studio (UI and installation), including how to start an InfoPath solution in Visual Studio 2008
- Creating an InfoPath solution—object model, and object model functional area
- Events in InfoPath—form-level events, XML events, and control events
- Custom programming—data validation, custom actions on save, and switching views
- Manipulating the Data Source—making InfoPath work with Microsoft SQL Server
- Creating a custom Task Pane for InfoPath 2007
- Writing InfoPath Add-ins using VSTO programming
- InfoPath and its important role in SharePoint Workflow

Microsoft Office InfoPath

When you design an InfoPath form, InfoPath creates a .xsn file, which is stored internally as a cabinet (.cab) file because it can actually contain additional subfiles. In other words, the .xsn file contains all of the necessary subfiles required to assist users in entering data and validating it.

There are two ways to see the files that are contained inside a .xsn file. The first approach is to open your .xsn InfoPath form in InfoPath designer. InfoPath designer is simply the Microsoft Office InfoPath 2007 form template design environment. The second approach requires a little more effort. You can rename your .xsn files to the .cab extension and then extract all of the files related to the original .xsn file to a specified folder. Microsoft Office InfoPath 2007 is based on an industry-standard Extensible Markup Language. This allows developers to create customized tags that offer flexibility in organizing and presenting information.

The simplicity of InfoPath forms solutions is that they provide support and facilitate you in combining multiform process information into a single electronic form using which you can gather all of the required information for your processes.

At this point, you might ask: if InfoPath is built into Microsoft Office, why are we discussing it as a part of Visual Studio? Here's why. Even though the InfoPath designer has remarkable features for creating forms with validation rules, a lot of design capabilities cannot be achieved using the standard InfoPath environment. When you find that you can't create the forms that you want by using the InfoPath designer, you would typically resort to scripting, or managed code, to achieve the functionality that you wanted. With both InfoPath and Visual Studio, that's not necessary. A Visual Studio tool for Office development provides an environment that allows you to integrate Visual Studio with Microsoft Office's InfoPath tools, to create a virtually limitless approach to forms creation.

InfoPath 2007 in Visual Studio

When Microsoft first released InfoPath, in 2003, the software had some serious limitations. There was no easy way to combine InfoPath with programming languages. As a result, there was no easy way to use a language to refine the functionality of a form that had been designed with InfoPath.

When Microsoft launched the Visual Studio 2005 edition, they also released a toolkit for InfoPath that allowed programmers to integrate Visual Studio and InfoPath, in order to create managed code solutions for Microsoft Office applications. Managed code is program code that executes under the supervision of a virtual environment. Programs in any language can be compiled either into managed code or unmanaged code. Here, the code built on a .NET framework is meant to be managed code.

The bottom line is that VSTO 3.0 is well-integrated with Visual Studio 2008. It provides .NET platform developers with tools for building applications that influence Microsoft Office InfoPath 2007 (and other Microsoft Office programs, such as Microsoft Excel 2007 and Microsoft Word 2007)—all in an environment that matches the development, deployment, and security of live .NET applications. Whenever you find that the features of the InfoPath form designer aren't robust enough to get the job done, you can write scripted or managed code to create your ideal InfoPath form. In Microsoft InfoPath, every control on a form must be bound to an element in the corresponding XML document.

 VSTO offers supporting tools that Office developers can use to build on top of Office applications as a platform.

Writing scripts for InfoPath is typically done in JavaScript, which unfortunately has a very limited set of features when you compare them with the functionality attainable with managed code such as C#. Managed code gives you many additional options, including creating plugins, more flexible form solutions, and much more.

Visual Studio 2008 InfoPath solution overview

The VSTO 3.0 experience brings InfoPath forms right into Visual Studio by using InfoPath 2007. Once you have installed Visual Studio 2008 in your development environment, you're ready to create InfoPath solutions by using Visual Studio. The following images in this section show the steps to the InfoPath solution using Visual Studio. These are the dialog boxes and the environment window that you will use when you begin creating InfoPath solutions.

The following screenshot displays Visual Studio **New Project** dialog box that you use to open an InfoPath template from Visual Studio.

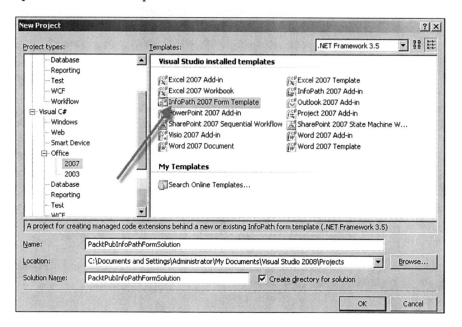

The next screenshot shows the **Design a Form Template** dialog box, in which you select the type of template that you want to create. The type of template that you select is normally determined based on your data source (database, XML file, and so on). You can also use this dialog box to open an existing form template.

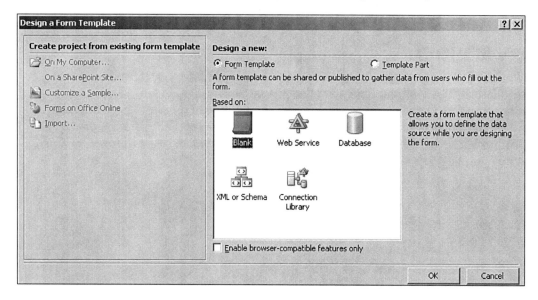

The window in the next screenshot shows all of the supporting files (in the rightmost pane) for creating an InfoPath solution. The `formcode.cs` file is used to write business logic, in other words, the customization code for your InfoPath solutions. This screenshot shows the InfoPath environment in Visual Studio 2008. **Web Service** is used to create forms that interact with the web service for data processing. A **Database** is used to create forms that interact with the Access or Microsoft SQL Server Database for data processing. **XML or Schema** is used to create forms that process the data source as the existing XML document or the XML schema. **Connection Library** will search the Microsoft Office server for the existing data connection that can be used for the form.

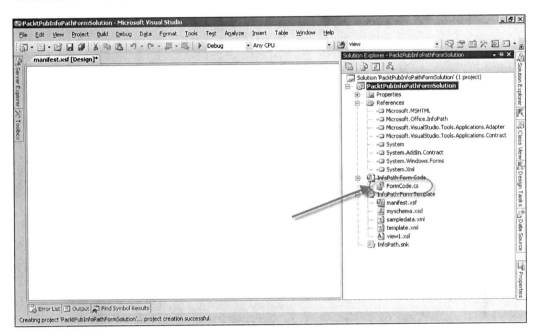

The VSTO problem when installing Office InfoPath 2007

When installing Microsoft Office InfoPath 2007, you need to carry out the following simple procedure to avoid the problem of programming compatibility with .NET framework:

1. Install the Microsoft Office 2007 clients (without .NET programming support for the .NET Framework version 2.0).

2. Install the .NET 3.0 Framework.

3. Install Microsoft Office SharePoint Portal Server 2007.
4. Go to **Add or Remove Programs** and add .NET programmability support for .NET Framework version 2.0.

Creating our first example

In our first example, we will make you more comfortable, by explaining the **Hello World** example using Visual Studio 2008 and Microsoft Office InfoPath 2007.

Let's write a **Hello World** program as our first program, using VSTO 3.0 for Microsoft InfoPath 2007.

1. Open Visual Studio 2008, and create a new **InfoPath 2007 Form** template project.
2. Select **New project**. Under **Office**, select **2007** and then select **InfoPath 2007 Form** template, and name the project as per your requirements.
3. Next, the **Design Template** dialog box appears. This is where you choose the template for your design requirement. In our example, we will select **Blank** and click on **OK**.
4. The solution will be created with all of supporting files for our development of InfoPath solution. Let's write a **Hello World** message on a button click event for an InfoPath form. In the design task pane of the Visual Studio window, you can find the **Controls** button hyper linked. The following screenshot shows the InfoPath Design Task Pane inside Visual Studio.

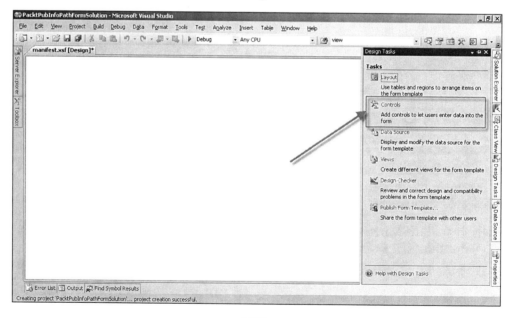

5. Next drag-and-drop a textbox to display the **Hello World** message and a button to write the `Click` event for, from InfoPath toolbox. The next image represents the InfoPath **Toolbox** Task Pane showing the InfoPath-supported controls.

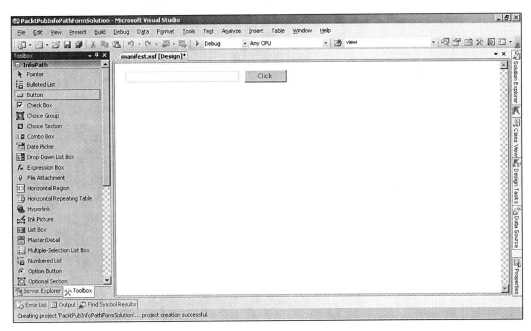

6. Right-click on the button and select **Button Properties** from the shortcut menu. In the **Button Properties** window, click on the **Edit Form Code** button under the **General** tab. This will generate the `Click` event for the button.

7. Add the following code into the control's `Click` event:

```
public void Click_Clicked(object sender, ClickedEventArgs e)
{
// Read the Textbox and write the "Hello World"
    XPathNavigator xNode = MainDataSource.CreateNavigator().
        SelectSingleNode("/my:myFields/my:field1",
        NamespaceManager);
    // Set value to Textbox
    xNode.SetValue("Hello World");
}
```

Once you have added and executed the above code, you will get the following screenshot as the output.

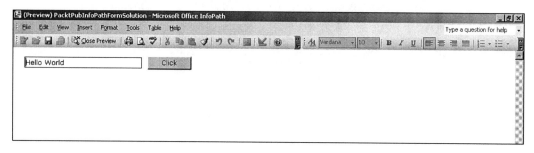

Available customization features

InfoPath programmability encourages you to customize an InfoPath form by altering its form files or by writing scripting code to create custom functions by using the InfoPath object model. The main components of an InfoPath form that support customization are:

- Data validation
- Event handling
- User interface
- Editing controls
- Error handling
- Security
- Data submission
- Business logic
- Form integration

Data validation

Data validation is the process of testing the correctness of entered data. You can apply a set of rules to a control or field to specify the type and range of data that users are allowed to enter. If a user enters an incorrect value into a form, data validation code will display error messages to users. With the support of data validation in InfoPath you can also write custom code to achieve complex validation.

 Microsoft Office InfoPath 2007 imposes the distinct XML schema whenever a user enters data in the InfoPath form; this is also known as schema validation.

InfoPath 2007 supports improved custom data validation through the use of managed code. Several new classes provide you with the ability to generate data validation errors for cases that previously couldn't be detected. With the use of these powerful InfoPath data validation capabilities, you can enforce business logic more thoroughly in your Office solutions.

Custom actions on save

Developing custom save functionality for an Office InfoPath 2007 form template is easy to achieve. The SaveEventArgs object can be used during a save operation (from an event handler for the Save event) to determine save properties and to perform the actual save operation. The SaveEventArgs object can be accessed only from code running in forms that were opened in Microsoft Office InfoPath 2007.

Switching views

Microsoft Office InfoPath forms support multiple views. When you open a form in InfoPath, the default view appears, which is based on the user's previous interaction and previously-implemented rules. Microsoft InfoPath provides the SwitchView method to allow you to shift views from inside the form through the use of managed code. The SwitchView method is activated from the View object, which in turn doesn't activate until the Loading event has completed. Here's a simple code example that shows how to switch views:

```
public void btnApply1_Clicked(object sender, ClickedEventArgs e)
{
    ViewInfos.SwitchView("ViewName");
}
```

The code shows that, on a button click, the view will be switched to the name of the view defined in the SwitchView method.

Object model in InfoPath solution

InfoPath forms are intended to be easy to use. The concept is that a simple form can be used by numerous people in a small workgroup to collect information. For example, a 25-person marketing team might use different instances of the same form to fill out and share information about client calls that the staff make. The data in these forms might then be merged into a single summary report that is sent to the management every month. On the other hand, InfoPath forms can be more dedicated, meaning they can be connected to existing databases, or integrated into existing business systems.

Let's suppose your company uses Microsoft SharePoint to manage the process of expense reporting; the developers in your IT department might design an InfoPath expense form that enables users to submit data directly to SharePoint, which in turn routes that data to the appropriate department for approval. One of the main advantages of Microsoft InfoPath 2007 is that you can use it to quickly create a frontend for your input form.

Understanding the Microsoft Office InfoPath object model

If you're eager to leverage Microsoft Office InfoPath functionality in enterprise software applications, you may be pleased to discover that the VSTO InfoPath object model provides most of the functionality of Microsoft Office InfoPath. The Microsoft Office InfoPath 2007 object model provides improved support for managed code when compared to the previous version of the VSTO InfoPath object model.

The Microsoft Office InfoPath object model is a **Component Object Model (COM)**. The importance of COM is that it is a language-neutral way of implementing objects that can be used in different environments. The InfoPath object model can be used to interact with InfoPath forms and their underlying XML documents. It is similar to other Microsoft Office application object models — the object model implements interfaces for collections, objects, properties, methods, and events.

The InfoPath 2007 object model is not supported in Microsoft Office InfoPath 2003. So, if you use the InfoPath 2007 object model to write code for your Microsoft Office InfoPath 2007 solution, and then decide to make that form template compatible with Microsoft Office InfoPath 2003, you must remove the code or rewrite it using the InfoPath 2003 object model.

When Microsoft launched InfoPath 2007, they added several new objects, collections, and enumerations to the existing object model.

Previously, in the InfoPath 2003 object model, objects were packed in three namespaces: `Microsoft.Office.InfoPath`, `Microsoft.Office.Interop.InfoPath`, and `Microsoft.Office.Interop.InfoPath.Xml`. In the new version, all objects and collections related to InfoPath are packed in the single namespace `Microsoft.Office.InfoPath`.

The following table provides a quick overview of the InfoPath object model. It shows the frequently-used objects whose names were changed depending on their usage in programming.

InfoPath 2003 object model	InfoPath 2007 object model
`thisXDocument.DOM`	`this.MainDataSource`
`IXMLDOMNode`	`XPathNavigator`
Read `field1.text`	Read `field1.Value`
Set `field1.text`	Set using `field1.SetValue()`

Understanding the InfoPath object model functional area

The InfoPath 2007 object model is designed in such a way that the same object model can be used for both client and server development environments. The InfoPath 2007 object model is a well-built hierarchical type library composed of classes, objects, collections, properties, methods, and events. The InfoPath object model supports Office developers in manipulating many parts of an InfoPath application or form template with the standard application programming interface.

The following are some of the InfoPath managed-code object model classes and objects:

- `Application`
- `WindowCollection`
- `Window`
- `XmlFormCollection`
- `XmlForm`
- `ViewInfoCollection`
- `View`

You can download the managed object model from MSDN. Search for **InfoPathObjectModelMap**. This document is useful to all Microsoft InfoPath developers.

Let's look at each of these components to determine how they fit into the object model.

Application

The base of the InfoPath 2007 object model is the `Application` class. The `Application` class includes properties and methods that return references to the high-level objects of the InfoPath object model. The `Application` object in the InfoPath object model provides a number of properties and methods that can be used not only to access lower-level collections and objects in the object model, but also to perform a variety of extended-use functions.

```
// Accessing the User property of the Application class and reading
    the logged in Username
    this.Application.User.UserName.ToString();
```

WindowCollection

`WindowCollection` contains a `Window` object for each window within a Microsoft Office InfoPath 2007 form. The `Windowcollection` implements properties that can be used to access a form's associated `Window` objects. It is accessible through the `Windows` property of the `Application` object. `WindowCollection` members have two core properties — `count` and `item`, which handle the property called `Windows` from the Windows collection. The `WindowCollection` collection can be used only to get the number of `Window` objects that the collection contains.

```
// Reference to the InfoPath WindowCollection and accessing the
    Application window

    Microsoft.Office.InfoPath.WindowCollection
        InfoPathWindowCollection = this.Application.Windows;
// Reading the count of InfoPath windows
    InfoPathWindowCollection.Count.ToString();
```

Window

The `Window` objects of an InfoPath form are accessed all the way through the `Item` property of the `WindowCollection` object. The `Application` class has a property for enumerating windows, which is a collection of `Window` objects. The `Window` object provides a number of properties and methods that can be used to programmatically interact with InfoPath windows. You can also access the `view` by using the windows' object properties. Views are an essential part of InfoPath forms.

Views are used to represent the data from the original data structures in a mixture of formats.

```
// Reference to InfoPath Window class and reading the
    ActiveWindow
    Window InfoPathWindow = this.Application.ActiveWindow;
```

```
// Getting the WindowState of the InfoPath example maximized,
    minimized or normal
    InfoPathWindow.WindowState.ToString();
```

XmlFormCollection

The XmlFormCollection object has the ability to access the current instance of InfoPath through the XmlForms property of the Application object. By using the XmlForm class, you can easily access form templates and form data.

```
// Reference to InfoPath XmlFormCollection in the Application
    XmlFormCollection InfoPathXmlFormCollection = this.Application.
                                                    XmlForms;
```

```
// Gets the count of the XmlFormCollection collection
    InfoPathXmlFormCollection.Count;
```

XmlForm

The XmlForm class represents the essential XML document of an InfoPath form. Also, the XmlForm class is one of the key objects in the InfoPath object model. The XmlForm class provides other properties that can be used to get information about the InfoPath form.

```
// Datasource navigation through XPath navigator
    XPathNavigator DataSourceNavigator = this.MainDataSource.
                                            CreateNavigator();
```

```
// Reading through the XML structure in the InfoPath XML form
    DataSourceNavigator.SelectSingleNode("/my:myFields/my:field1",
                                        this.NamespaceManager);
```

```
// Setting the value for the field in XML form
    SetValue("Demo for XmlForm Class");
```

View

The View class represents the view (appearance) of the InfoPath form. The View class provides the ViewInfo property, which allows you to access information about the associated view. The ForceUpdate method is one of the most useful methods, and updates the current view programmatically.

```
// Reference to InfoPath View class and reading the CurrentView
      property
    Microsoft.Office.InfoPath.View InfoPathView = this.CurrentView;
```

```
// Reading the Caption of the current view
    InfoPathView.ViewInfo.Caption.ToString();
```

ViewInfoCollection

The ViewInfoCollection object for an InfoPath form can be accessed through the ViewInfos property of the XmlForm class. The ViewInfoCollection class contains a ViewInfo object for each view within a form. Also, the ViewInfoCollection class implements properties that can be used to access the ViewInfo object associated with each view in a form. For example, the CurrentView property returns a View object that describes the current view of the InfoPath form.

```
// Referencing the ViewInfoCollection class of InfoPath form
    ViewInfoCollection ReadViewInformation = this.ViewInfos;
// Reading through the properties of the variable ReadViewInformation
    ReadViewInformation.Default.Name.ToString();
```

Using events in InfoPath

The events available to InfoPath developers in Microsoft InfoPath 2007 are different from the events available to other technology forms developers. For example, the InfoPath hosted control, provided by the InfoPath event manager, gives the developers of third-party hosted applications the ability to respond to events defined in the form. The InfoPath event manager provides this functionality.

[Event names are case sensitive, unlike those in HTML or XHTML forms.]

InfoPath 2007 events can be classified into the following three types:

- Form-level events
- XML and data validation events
- Control events

Form-level events

You can write code to react to different events that can occur in Microsoft Office InfoPath 2007, as a user fills out a form. In InfoPath, events take the form of event handlers that are created when you work with a form in design mode. InfoPath event handlers must be initially created in design mode because, in addition to the scripting declarations that are created in a form's primary scripting file, entries are also made in the form definition (.xsf) file. After you have created an event handler, you should not alter its declaration in the primary scripting file. The following table describes how each form-level event behaves.

Name	Description
FormEvents_Loading()	Returns a reference to a form's essential XML document and return status during the loading of a form; the Loading event is bound using the LoadingEventHandler delegate
FormEvents_ViewSwitched()	Returns a reference to a form's essential XML document during a switch view operation; the ViewSwitched event is bound using the ViewSwitchedEventHandler delegate
FormEvents_ContextChanged()	Returns information about the XML **Document Object Model (DOM)** node that is the current context of the form's essential XML document; the ContextChanged event is bound using the ContextChangedEventHandler delegate
FormEvents_Submit()	Used to prevent the form from being submitted if the form has not been saved first; the Submit event is activated only if the form template has the Perform Custom Action Using Code option set in the Submit Options dialog box; the Submit event is bound using the SubmitEventHandler delegate
FormEvents_VersionUpgrade()	An event handler for the VersionUpgrade event, which allows you to run the code to update a form when the form template on which it is based has been upgraded since the form was last opened; the event handler is used to display the version numbers of the form and form template; the VersionUpgrade event is bound using the VersionUpgradeEventHandler delegate

Name	Description
FormEvents_Save()	The event handler for the Save event, where we should insert any pre-defined business logic to determine whether all data has been entered according to defined rules; if the data is determined to be valid, this event handler performs a save; if any invalid entries are found, the event handler displays a message and cancels the save operation; the Save event is activated only if the form template has the Save Using Custom Code option set in the Form Options dialog box; the Save event is bound using the SaveEventHandler delegate
FormEvents_Sign()	Used to add additional data to a digital signature; this event handler will run only in fully-trusted form templates; the Sign event is bound using the SignEventHandler delegate
FormEvents_Merge()	Returns properties and methods that can be used during a Merge event to programmatically interact with a form's essential XML document and to determine merge properties, such as the number of files being merged; the Merge event is bound using the MergeEventHandler delegate

 A delegate is a member of a group, which represents the same group. A delegate is an object that refers to a static method or an instance of a method.

To receive events when a form is processed, you need to first register the events. You can use the InternalStartup method to add code to register the events. The InternalStartup method is generated by the IDE. Events can be registered either manually or using the IDE. For form-level events, the code displays the following:

```
// Note that the following procedure is required by Microsoft Office
   InfoPath.
// It can be modified using Microsoft Office InfoPath.
public void InternalStartup()
{
    EventManager.FormEvents.Loading += new
        LoadingEventHandler(FormEvents_Loading);
}
```

If you receive the following error message while running your InfoPath solution from Visual Studio 2008: **Microsoft Office InfoPath does not recognize some or all of the command line options. Exit and restart Microsoft Office InfoPath with the correct command line options**— you need to update your Office tools with the latest service-pack release.

Here's another way to register events. First, open your form in InfoPath Designer, which is located inside the **Solution** folder that shows the list of files. The folder and the file structure will be the same for all InfoPath solutions created using Visual Studio 2008, as shown in the following image:

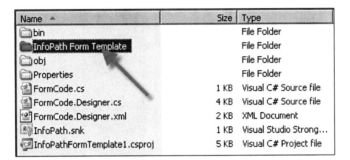

The **Microsoft Form Definition File** (the `manifest.xsf` file) is located inside the **InfoPath Form Template** folder, the contents of which are shown in the following screenshot:

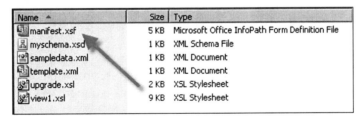

Open the `manifest.xsf` file in the InfoPath designer, to register events. Click through the sequence of menu items available in the InfoPath designer tool, as shown in the following screenshot:

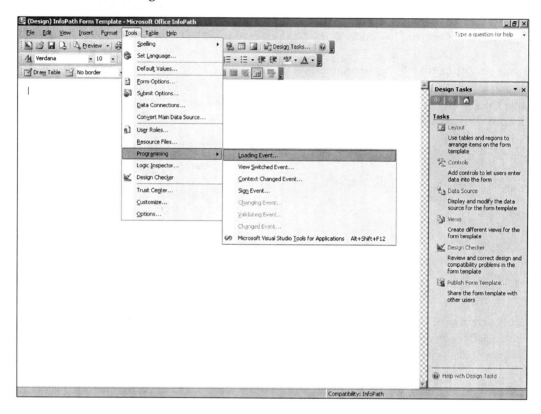

The previous screenshot shows the sequence of menu items used to access form-level events from the **Tools** menu. In this example, you click on the **Tools** menu, and then select **Programming** from the drop-down menu. Notice that some events are enabled, while some are disabled (greyed out). Next, click on the name of the event that you want to register (in this example, **Loading Event...**).

> If an XML node includes the attribute `xsi:nil="true"`, any text value of the XML node will produce XML that is not valid. As a result, Microsoft Office InfoPath will not accept the value, and you will receive an error message when you try to set it. To work around this problem, simply add the code that checks for the `xsi:nil="true"` attribute. InfoPath will then remove the attribute at run time—before the code sets the text value of the node. To see how this works, take a look at the following example.

An example of the solution xsi:nil="true" attribute

Microsoft Office InfoPath forms are prepared by connecting to a **Web Service Contract-First (WSCF)** web services. When you examine the schemas, you will not find the nullable attribute that equals `"true"` in the **XML Schema Definition (XSD)** generated (`.XSD` file) by InfoPath. The XSD is referred to as the XML Schema language. `xsi:nil="true"` is the nullable attribute that we need to handle in the InfoPath.

```
// Create a Navigator object to access the main DOM.
    XPathNavigator xDoc = this.MainDataSource.CreateNavigator();
// Create a Navigator object for the field that you want to set.
    XPathNavigator xData = xDoc.
        SelectSingleNode("/my:myFields/my:myName",
        this.NamespaceManager);
// Check and remove the "nil" attribute.
    if (xData.MoveToAttribute("nil", "http://www.w3.org/2001/XMLSchema
        -instance"))
    xData.DeleteSelf();
// Set the value of the myName field.
    xData.SetValue("Vivek");
// Data clean up.
    xDoc = null;
    xData = null;
```

The following sections describe the use of the events that you can select from the **Programming** submenu.

Loading event

After you work through the menu options shown in the previous image, an event handler will be created in your code to handle the specific event. Let's work through a sample to see how the `Loading` event works in the InfoPath form.

```
FormEvents_Loading(object sender, LoadingEventArgs e)
```

The following example will load information about the currently logged-in user. The form will display the user's name by returning this information from the `Loading` event.

```
public void FormEvents_Loading(object sender, LoadingEventArgs e)
{
// Create a Navigator object to access the main DOM
    XPathNavigator xDoc = this.MainDataSource.CreateNavigator();
// Create a Navigator object for the field that you want to set
```

```
    XPathNavigator xData = xDoc.SelectSingleNode("/my:
        myFields/my:field1", this.NamespaceManager);
// Check and remove the "nil" attribute
    if (xData.MoveToAttribute("nil",
        "http://www.w3.org/2001/XMLSchema-instance"))
    xData.DeleteSelf();
// Loading the current user's name into a string variable
    string strLoggedInUserName = System.Environment.UserName;
// Assigning the user'sname to the field value
    xData.SetValue(strLoggedInUserName);
}
```

The `Loading` event can be cancelled by using the `CancelableArgs` property of the `SaveEventArgs` class and then setting the `Cancel` property to "true".

Using the ViewSwitched event

By using the InfoPath form's `ViewSwitched` event, you can sync to other form events such as `Save`, `Merge`, and so on.

```
FormEvents_ViewSwitched(object sender, ViewSwitchedEventArgs e)
```

InfoPath Forms Services is a server technology that makes it possible for users to fill out InfoPath forms in a web browser.

```
public void FormEvents_ViewSwitched(object sender,
    ViewSwitchedEventArgs e)
{
// Messagebox will display the view name with custom message
    MessageBox.Show("Currently loading the view named: " +
        this.CurrentView.ViewInfo.Name);
}
```

Using the ContextChanged event

The `ContextChanged` event occurs when the context node changes. The `ContextChanged` event is not supported in browser-enabled forms. Browser-enabled forms are designed in InfoPath and can be filled out either in InfoPath or in a web browser. InfoPath browser-enabled forms are to be used for better performance and scalability. In addition, note that the `ContextChanged` event is asynchronous — the event is not activated on every change in the context node; instead, it is activated after the application has stopped processing other events.

```
FormEvents_ContextChanged(object sender, ContextChangedEventArgs e)
```

Here's an example of the `ContextChanged` event.

```
public void FormEvents_ContextChanged(object sender,
    ContextChangedEventArgs e)
{
    if (e.ChangeType == "ContextNode")
    {
    // Position a XPathNavigator on the DisplayContext field.
        XPathNavigator rtNode, msgTxtBox;
        rtNode = this.MainDataSource.CreateNavigator();
        msgTxtBox = rtNode.SelectSingleNode("/my:myFields/my:field2",
            this.NamespaceManager);
    // Set DisplayContext with the name of the current context.
        msgTxtBox.SetValue("Context Name: " + e.Context.Name + ",
            Context Type: " + e.Context.NodeType);
    //Even you can change the view on context change
    //Switching view after the context change
        ViewInfos.SwitchView("Context Changed");
        return;
    }
}
```

Using the Submit event

If your InfoPath form is also on a hosted Microsoft Office InfoPath 2007 form that uses the `Submit` event handler, the `Submit` event always occurs first in the InfoPath form and then in the host form.

```
FormEvents_Submit(object sender, SubmitEventArgs e)
```

If the code in the `Submit` event in InfoPath 2007 cancels the event due to an error, the `Submit` event in the host form will not occur, and the user may receive an error message stating that **The form cannot be submitted.** The following code demonstrates the use of the `Submit` event.

```
private bool Validate()
{
    string strAge = MainDataSource.CreateNavigator().
                    SelectSingleNode("/my:myFields/my:MyAge",
                    NamespaceManager).InnerXml;
    if (strAge.Length == 0)
    {
        MessageBox.Show("Please enter your age!");
        return false;
    }
    return true;
}
public void FormEvents_Submit(object sender, SubmitEventArgs e)
{
```

```
    if (Validate() == true)
    {
        string xPath = "/my:myFields/my:MyAge";
        XPathNavigator xNavigator = MainDataSource.CreateNavigator();
        XPathNavigator xValueNavigator = xNavigator.
            SelectSingleNode(xPath, NamespaceManager);
        FileSubmitConnection xConnection = (FileSubmitConnection)(
            DataConnections["DataSource"]); xConnection.
            Execute(xValueNavigator);
    }
    else
    {
        MessageBox.Show("Please fill the form correctly");
    }
}
```

Using the VersionUpgrade event

The `VersionUpgrade` events are not available from third-party hosted applications because these events occur before the form is loaded in the hosted application.

```
FormEvents_VersionUpgrade(object sender, VersionUpgradeEventArgs e)
```

This event is triggered when the version number of the form being opened is older than the version number of the form template on which it is based. Here's an example:

```
public void FormEvents_VersionUpgrade(object sender,
    VersionUpgradeEventArgs e)
{
// Version details displayed in Message box
    MessageBox.Show("InfoPath Form Version: " + e.DocumentVersion +
                    "\n InfoPath Form Template Version: " +
                    e.FormTemplateVersion);
}
```

The `VersionUpgrade` event can be cancelled by using the `CancelableArgs` property of the `VersionUpgradeEventArgs` class to set the `Cancel` property to `true`.

Using the Save event

The `Save` event is not meant to be instantiated by the developer in form code. You can add event handlers for form-level events via the Microsoft Office InfoPath 2007 Design mode user interface.

```
FormEvents_Save(object sender, SaveEventArgs e)
```

The `SaveEventArgs` object, which is passed as a parameter to an event handler for the `Save` event, provides properties and methods that can be used to get the form's file name, determine the `Save` status, and perform the `Save` operation.

To add a custom `Save` event to the **InfoPath Form** template, follow these steps:

1. Open the **Tools** menu and click on **Form Options**.
2. In the **Form Options** dialog box, click on **Open and Save category**, select the **Save using custom code** checkbox, and then click on **Edit**.
3. Click **OK** to close the **Form Options** dialog box, and then replace the contents of the `FormEvents_Save` method with the following code sample:

```
public void FormEvents_Save(object sender, SaveEventArgs e)
{
// Read the node
    string strBookName = MainDataSource.CreateNavigator().
        SelectSingleNode("/my:myFields/my:BookName",
        NamespaceManager).InnerXml;

// Check the BookName enetered in the textbox
if (strBookName == string.Empty)
{
// If textbox is empty, prompt message to user
    e.CancelableArgs.Message = "Please enter the BookName to save
                                the Form";
    e.CancelableArgs.Cancel = true;
  }
else
{
// Open SaveAs dialog box
    if (e.IsSaveAs)
    {
        SetSaveAsDialogFilename(strBookName + ".xml");
    }
    e.PerformSaveOperation();
    e.CancelableArgs.Cancel = false;
  }
}
```

The following screenshot shows the InfoPath form:

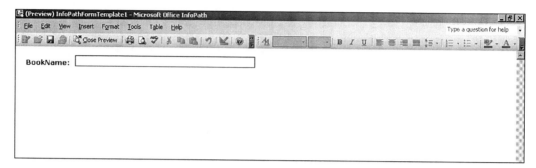

The next screenshot shows the InfoPath form prompt that appears when you try to save the form without entering the book name correctly in the text box shown in the previous screenshot.

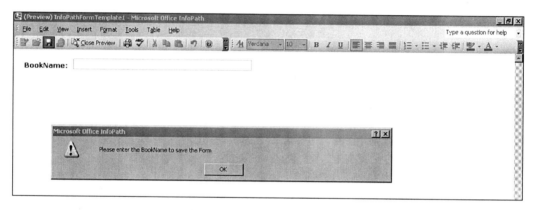

The form is in preview mode after the custom save has been implemented in the InfoPath solution.

The previous screenshot showed the dialog box that requests a book name for the form in preview mode — after the custom save has been implemented as an InfoPath solution. The following screenshot demonstrates how you can custom-save code in an InfoPath 2007 form.

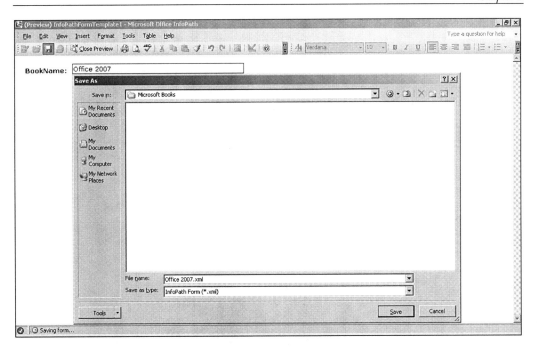

After the user enters the correct book name, InfoPath displays the **Save As** dialog box, as seen in the preceding screenshot, to save the InfoPath's data file to the desired location.

Sign event

The Sign event will take place only when the form can be completely trusted. In other words, an event handler for this event needs to confirm the **Full Trust** security level before it can run. You can use the event handler for the Sign event to add additional data to the digital signature.

```
FormEvents_Sign(object sender, SignEventArgs e)
```

Here's one easy way to add a signature—use the **Digital Signatures** dialog box, which you can access from the **Tools** menu. Older versions of InfoPath stored state values as hidden variables. InfoPath 2007 has a new property called FormState, which can be used to store state values. In the older versions of InfoPath, you had to use hidden variables. The FormState property reduces or eliminates the use of hidden variables. Hidden variables are variables that are used as holding places for values that can be read through programming. FormState is an IDictionary object, that holds user-defined state values defined in the variable declaration section.

```
// Constant declaration for sign status
    const string _signStatus = "Allowed";
```

```
//Form sign status property
private bool SignStatus
{
    get
    {
    // To store the state values FormState
        if (FormState.Contains(_signStatus))
        {
            return (bool)FormState[_signStatus];
        }
        return false;
    }
    set
    {
        if (!FormState.Contains(_signStatus))
        {
            FormState.Add(_signStatus, value);
        }
        else
        {
            FormState[_signStatus] = value;
        }
    }
}

public void FormEvents_Sign(object sender, SignEventArgs e)
{
// Form status check
    if (SignStatus)
    {
        Signature thisSignature = e.SignedDataBlock.Signatures.
            CreateSignature();
        thisSignature.Sign();
        e.SignatureWizard = true;
    }
    else
    {
        e.SignatureWizard = false;
        MessageBox.Show("Click here to proceed.");
        return;
    }
}
```

Merge event

In InfoPath 2003, you needed to write your own .xsl transformation code to perform a merge. In InfoPath 2007, merging forms can be done using a built-in event handler.

```
FormEvents_Merge(object sender, MergeEventArgs e)
```

Here is an example to show how the InfoPath forms can be merged:

```
public void FormEvents_Merge(object sender, MergeEventArgs e)
{
    string strFromPath = @"C:\InfoPathForm\Form1.xml";
    XmlDocument InfoPathXML = new XmlDocument();
// The InfoPath Form template must be Fully Trusted.
    InfoPathXML.Load(strFromPath);
    XPathNavigator xNavigate = InfoPathXML.CreateNavigator();
// Merge the root node to the current form.
    this.MergeForm(xNavigate);
}
```

A Merge event can be cancelled by using the CancelableArgs property of the MergeEventArgs class and setting the Cancel property to true.

Xml events

InfoPath 2007 is a powerful data-driven platform. XML events are otherwise called data validation events in InfoPath. The changed event, changing event, and the validating event are the events used for form validation purposes, as explained in the following table:

Name	Description
fieldname_Changed	Changed event will be fired after the changes to a form's essential XML document have been accepted and the Validating event has occurred; the Changed event is bound using the XmlChangedEventHandler delegate.
fieldname_Changing	Changing event will be fired after changes to a form's essential XML document have been made, but before the changes have been accepted; the Changing event is bound using the XmlChangingEventHandler delegate
fieldname_Validating	Validating event is fired after changes to a form's essential XML document have been accepted, but before the Changed event has occurred; the Validating event is bound using the XmlValidatingEventHandler delegate

Changed event

The InfoPath Changed event is activated when the form (or elements on the InfoPath form) has been changed.

```
fieldname_Changed(object sender, XmlEventArgs e)
```

The Changed event is normally used for changing data in an InfoPath form corresponding to other changes happening in the same InfoPath form. Consider an example where, once the total is changed, the message gets written to the user interface with both the old value and the new value. We write the functionality for the changed event of the field, as shown below.

```
public void fieldname_Changed(object sender, XmlEventArgs e)
{
    string StrManagerName = "";
// Check if value has changed and not a table insertion
    if (e.Operation == XmlOperation.ValueChange)
    {
// Get Current Row
        XPathNavigator xNavigator = e.Site;
        bool bParent = xNavigator.MoveToParent();
// Get Reference to the Gross Value
        XPathNavigator xField = xNavigator.SelectSingleNode("/my:
            Report/my:Total/my:grandtotal", this.NamespaceManager);
        StrValue = xField.InnerXml;
// Create a Navigator object to access the main DOM
        XPathNavigator xDoc = this.MainDataSource.CreateNavigator();
// Create a Navigator object for the field that you want to set
        XPathNavigator xData = xDoc.SelectSingleNode("/my:Report
            /my:Total/my:msgChange", this.NamespaceManager);
// Set old and newly changed manager names
        xData.SetValue("Old Total: " + e.OldValue.ToString() + " &
            New Value: " + e.NewValue.ToString());
    }
}
```

Changing event

You can use the Changing event to address advanced data validation requirements. This event occurs after the Validate event is activated. During the Changing event, the form's underlying XML document is placed in read-only mode.

```
fieldname_Changing(object sender, XmlChangingEventArgs e)
```

If the code detects an error, InfoPath rejects the user's changes and restores the data to its previous state. Here's an example:

```
public void myYearsOfExperience_Changing(object sender,
    XmlChangingEventArgs e)
{
    string strYearsOfExp = e.Site.SelectSingleNode("..
        /my:myYearsOfExperience", NamespaceManager).InnerXml;

    if (strYearsOfExp == string.Empty || strYearsOfExp == "")
    {
        e.CancelableArgs.Message = "Please enter a valid input";
        e.CancelableArgs.Cancel = true;
    }
}
```

Validating event

The InfoPath Validating event displays a prompt (if an error is found) before the form has finished loading.

```
fieldname_Validating(object sender, XmlValidatingEventArgs e)
```

In other words, the Validating event is normally used more for error handling in the InfoPath form, as compared to the data validation of the InfoPath form.

```
public void Name_Validating(object sender, XmlValidatingEventArgs e)
{
    XPathNavigator xNode = this.CreateNavigator().
        SelectSingleNode("/my:myFields/my:Name",NamespaceManager);
    this.Errors.Add(xNode, "Name to validate..", "error occured",
        "Correct the error");
}
```

Control events

InfoPath supports only one event when a button control is activated. The Clicked event is activated when a button control on a form is clicked, and is used to display a message to the user.

Clicked event

The following code uses the Clicked event to display the date and time when the user clicks on a particular button:

```
ButtonName_Clicked(object sender, ClickedEventArgs e)
```

The event handler for this event does not allow the user to cancel the event.

```
// Example for Click event to display date information.
public void btn_ClickEvent_Clicked(object sender, ClickedEventArgs e)
{
// Click event shows the message as current date.
    System.DateTime sysDate = new DateTime();
    MessageBox.Show(sysDate.Date.ToString());
}
```

Writing event validation for an expense report form

Let's work on a sample form and use some of the events available in Microsoft Office InfoPath 2007. Let's start by creating a company expense report form, and implementing the events for the validation of the user interface.

We are using most of the events available in InfoPath 2007 in the expense report for some of the user interface validation.

1. Start Microsoft Visual Studio 2008.
2. On the **File** menu, click on **New Project**.
3. In the **New Project** dialog box, expand **Visual C# project types**.
4. Select **New project**. Under **Office** select **2007**, and select **InfoPath 2007 Form** template. Name the project as per your requirements.
5. The **Design Template** dialog box is displayed. This is where you choose the appropriate template for your design. In this example, we have selected the **Expense Report** template.
6. Add the following code into the `formcode.cs` file.

```
public partial class FormCode
{
public void InternalStartup()
{
    EventManager.FormEvents.Loading += new
        LoadingEventHandler(FormEvents_Loading);
    EventManager.FormEvents.ContextChanged += new
        ContextChangedEventHandler(FormEvents_ContextChanged);
    EventManager.XmlEvents["/my:expenseReport/my:manager/
        my:managerEmailAddress"].Changing += new
        XmlChangingEventHandler(managerEmailAddress_Changing);
    EventManager.XmlEvents["/my:expenseReport/my:manager/
        my:managerName"].Changed += new
```

```
                XmlChangedEventHandler(managerName_Changed);
            ((ButtonEvent)EventManager.ControlEvents["
                Button_Submit"]).Clicked += new
                ClickedEventHandler(Button_Submit_Clicked);
    }
public void FormEvents_Loading(object sender, LoadingEventArgs e)
{
//Create a Navigator object to access the main DOM
    XPathNavigator xDoc = this.MainDataSource.CreateNavigator();
//Create a Navigator object for the field that you want to set
    XPathNavigator xData = xDoc.SelectSingleNode("/my:expenseReport/
        my:reportDate", this.NamespaceManager);

//Check and remove the "nil" attribute
    if (xData.MoveToAttribute("nil", "http://www.w3.org/2001/
        XMLSchema-instance"))
        xData.DeleteSelf();
}
public void FormEvents_ContextChanged(object sender,
    ContextChangedEventArgs e)
{
    if (e.ChangeType == "ContextNode")
    {
    // Position a XPathNavigator on the DisplayContext field.
        XPathNavigator rtNode, msgTxtBox;
        rtNode = this.MainDataSource.CreateNavigator();
        msgTxtBox = rtNode.SelectSingleNode("/my:expenseReport/
            my:manager/my:managerEmailAddress",
            this.NamespaceManager);

    //Create a Navigator object to access the main DOM
        XPathNavigator xDoc = this.MainDataSource.CreateNavigator();
    //Create a Navigator object for the field that you want to set
        XPathNavigator xData = xDoc.SelectSingleNode("/my:
            expenseReport/my:emailMessage", this.NamespaceManager);

    // Set DisplayContext with the name of the current context
        xData.SetValue("Current Context Name: " + e.Context.Name);

        return;
    }
}
public void managerEmailAddress_Changing(object sender,
    XmlChangingEventArgs e)
{
```

```
// Ensure that the constraint you are enforcing is compatible
// With the default value you set for this XML node.
    string strManagerEmail = e.Site.SelectSingleNode("/my:
        expenseReport/my:manager/my:managerEmailAddress",
        NamespaceManager).InnerXml;

// valiadting the Email format
    if (!isEmail(strManagerEmail))
    {
        if (strManagerEmail == string.Empty || strManagerEmail == "")
        {
         // Validation message
            e.CancelableArgs.Message = "Please enter a valid
                E-Mail";
            e.CancelableArgs.Cancel = true;
        }
    }
}

// Function to validate Email
public static bool isEmail(string inputEmail)
{
// Regular expression for Email
    string strRegex = @"^([a-zA-Z0-9_\-\.]+)@((\[[0-9]{1,3}" +
        @"\.[0-9]{1,3}\.[0-9]{1,3}\.)|(([a-zA-Z0-9\-]+\" +
        @".)+))([a-zA-Z]{2,4}|[0-9]{1,3})(\]?)$";

    Regex reg = new Regex(strRegex);
// Compare the regular expression
    if (reg.IsMatch(inputEmail))
        return (true);
    else
        return (false);
}

public void managerName_Changed(object sender, XmlEventArgs e)
{
    string StrManagerName = "";
// Check if value has changed and not a table insertion
    if (e.Operation == XmlOperation.ValueChange)
    {
    // Get Current Row
        XPathNavigator xNavigator = e.Site;
        bool bParent = xNavigator.MoveToParent();

    // Get Reference to the Gross Value
```

```
        XPathNavigator xField = xNavigator.SelectSingleNode("/my:
            expenseReport/my:manager/my:managerName",
            this.NamespaceManager);
        StrManagerName = xField.InnerXml;

    //Create a Navigator object to access the main DOM
        XPathNavigator xDoc = this.MainDataSource.CreateNavigator();

    //Create a Navigator object for the field that you want to set
        XPathNavigator xData = xDoc.SelectSingleNode("/my:
            expenseReport/my:msgManagerChange", this.NamespaceManager);

    // Set old and newly changed manager names
        xData.SetValue("Old Name: " + e.OldValue.ToString() + " & New
            Name: " + e.NewValue.ToString());

    }
}

public void Button_Submit_Clicked(object sender, ClickedEventArgs e)
{
    XPathNavigator xNavigator = this.MainDataSource.
        CreateNavigator();
// Primary value to be validated
    XPathNavigator xMgrValue = xNavigator.SelectSingleNode("/my:
        expenseReport/my:manager/my:managerName",
        this.NamespaceManager);
    XPathNavigator xMgrEmailValue = xNavigator.SelectSingleNode("/my:
        expenseReport/my:manager/my:managerEmailAddress",
        this.NamespaceManager);

        if (xMgrValue.Value.ToString() == string.Empty ||
            xMgrEmailValue.Value.ToString() == string.Empty)
        {
            MessageBox.Show("Please enter manager information");
        }
    }
}
```

Now, you can see the following screenshots as a result of executing the preceding code:

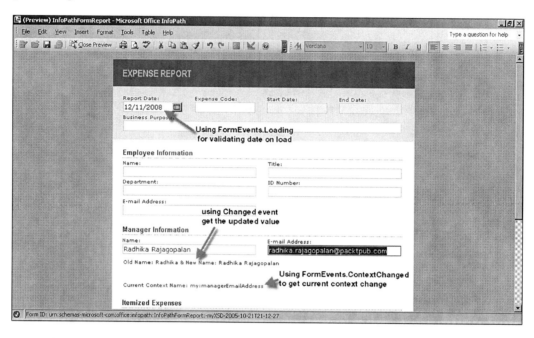

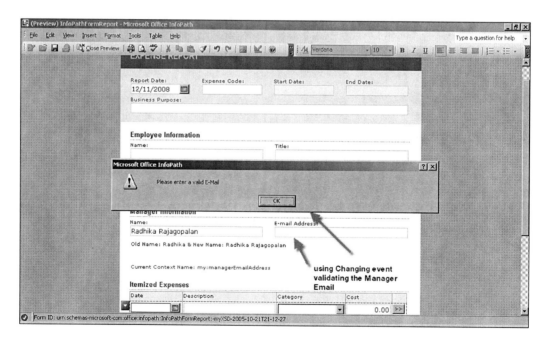

Manipulating a data source

There may be some reason or requirement for the developer to interact with data source from the code, that is, for manipulating a data source from managed code. A data source is a data structure that has information about a specific data file or database. We may have different requirements, such as manipulating data using the data source information. Or we may need to work extensively on a process before sending it to a data source. Anything like this may need various kinds of data source interaction using code.

Let's take a different scenario—how Microsoft SQL Server connects to InfoPath and manipulates the data in the InfoPath form and explain it by way of a demonstration. Populating InfoPath form fields with data returned by the SQL database is not a difficult task, but the scenario is how we are going to manipulate the secondary data source from inside the InfoPath form, and how we are going to manage the data inside the form. And this is not the only scenario to explain how the data source data can be manipulated; this is only one of those scenarios.

Fetch node value from main data source

One of the more important processes in an InfoPath managed code solution is the ability to retrieve a single node from an XML data source.

In our demonstration, let's take a look at how a single node value can be retrieved using a custom function in C#, which returns the value in the string format. Here, the FetchSingleNodeValue_MainDataSource function returns a string value when passed a single XPath statement argument.

```
// Custom function to fetch the single node from the main data source.
private string FetchSingleNodeValue_MainDataSource(string xPath)
{
// Navigate through main data source
    XPathNavigator xNode = MainDataSource.CreateNavigator().
        SelectSingleNode(xPath, NamespaceManager);
    return xNode.ToString();
}
// Button click event to call the custom function and display the
result.
public void btn_nodevalue_Clicked(object sender, ClickedEventArgs e)
{
// Call the custom function to result the data.
    string strResult = FetchSingleNodeValue_MainDataSource("/my:
        myFields/my:myName");
    MessageBox.Show(strResult);
}
```

In some cases, the node value that your program is trying to retrieve will be relative to a particular event object. In the `FetchSingleNodeValue_MainDataSource` function, the event object is passed as an argument along with the `XPath` statement to override this situation.

```
// Custom function to fetch the single node from main data source.
private string FetchSingleNodeValue_MainDataSource(string xPath,
    XmlEventArgs objEventArg)
{
    // Navigate through main data source using XMLeventarg.
    XPathNavigator xNode = objEventArg.Site.SelectSingleNode(xPath,
        NamespaceManager);
    return xNode.ToString();
}
```

Assigning a value to a node in the main data source

The `AssignNodeValue_ToMainDataSource` function uses the first `XPath` statement argument to identify an `XPathNavigator` object, and then assigns it to the value of the second argument.

```
// Custom function
private string AssignNodeValue_ToMainDataSource(string xPath,
    string strValue)
{
// Navigate through main data source
    XPathNavigator xNode = MainDataSource.CreateNavigator().
        SelectSingleNode(xPath, NamespaceManager);
    xNode.SetValue(strValue);
    return xNode.ToString();
}

// Button click event
public void btn_SetNodeValue_Clicked(object sender,
    ClickedEventArgs e)
{
// Call the custom function to result the data & Passing parameter
    string strResult = AssignNodeValue_ToMainDataSource("/my:
        myFields/my:myChapterName", "Programming InfoPath");
    MessageBox.Show("Assigned value is : " + strResult);
}
```

Adding or creating a new node in the main data source

An XML structure within an InfoPath form can include an internal recurring section or a recurring table control. Suppose that you want to add a row to a recurring section or a recurring table while some user action occurs or while a form is loading. You can achieve this by applying the XPathNavigator object in conjunction with the InsertAfter or AppendChildElement methods. In the following example, we create a new node through the use of the button click event.

```
public void btn_addrow_Clicked(object sender, ClickedEventArgs e)
{
// Get a reference to the node the repeating table is bound to
    XPathNavigator xNav = MainDataSource.CreateNavigator().
        SelectSingleNode("/my:myFields/my:group1/my:group2",
        this.NamespaceManager);
// Make a copy of the node by cloning it
    XPathNavigator xRow = xNav.Clone();
// Set the new values of the row's fields
    xRow.SelectSingleNode("/my:myFields/my:group1/my:group2/my:
        field1", this.NamespaceManager);
    xRow.SelectSingleNode("/my:myFields/my:group1/my:group2/my:
        field2", this.NamespaceManager);
    xRow.SelectSingleNode("/my:myFields/my:group1/my:group2/my:
        field3", this.NamespaceManager);
// Insert the new row after the last row in the table
    xNav.InsertAfter(xRow);
}
```

Whenever we click on the **AddRow** button, a new row gets created as shown in the following screenshot:

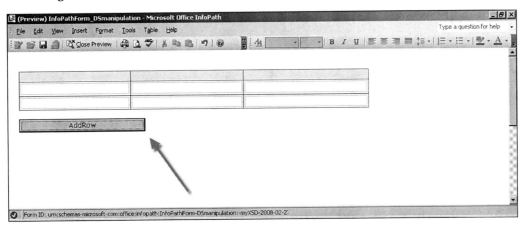

Deleting or removing nodes from the main data source

In the previous section, we saw how you can add a row to a recurring section or recurring table during user interaction, or while a form is loading. Similarly, you might also want to remove a node from a recurring section or recurring table.

To do so, you need to specify a row identity so that the program knows which row has been selected. In the following example, we use an radio button in the user interface. Here's the code to delete or remove a row:

```
public void btn_removeRow_Clicked(object sender, ClickedEventArgs e)
{
// Get a reference to the node the repeating table is bound to
    XPathNavigator xNav = MainDataSource.CreateNavigator().
        SelectSingleNode("/my:myFields/my:group3/my:group4",
        this.NamespaceManager);
// Get radio button value
    string rdValueCheck = xNav.SelectSingleNode("/my:myFields/my:
        group3/my:group4/my:rdBtnSelect",
        this.NamespaceManager).Value;
    if (rdValueCheck == "1")
    {
        xNav.DeleteSelf();
    }
}
```

When the user clicks the **RemoveRow** button, after selecting a row, the selected row will be removed.

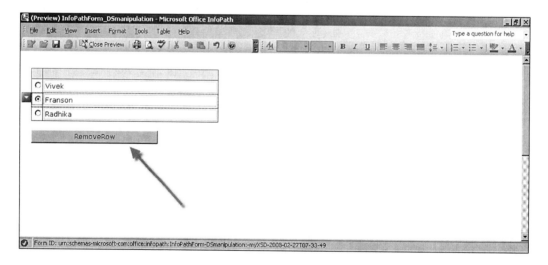

Populating Microsoft Office InfoPath with Microsoft SQL Server 2008

Now, let's take a look at how to connect Microsoft Office InfoPath 2007 to Microsoft SQL Server 2008 and populate InfoPath fields with data from a Microsoft SQL Server database. Connecting to a Microsoft SQL Server database is not a complex task in InfoPath. Using the data connection wizard, you can achieve this in a very simple way. In some scenarios, this process will not be sufficient to satisfy your business requirements. If this is the case, then you may have to go for custom coding. Using custom programming, you can connect to Microsoft SQL Server database, and manage, manipulate, and validate data. Let's see how to connect to Microsoft SQL Server 2008 and display data from a Microsoft SQL Server database in the InfoPath fields.

1. Start Microsoft Visual Studio 2008.

2. On the **File** menu, click on **New Project**.

3. In the **New Project** dialog box, expand **Visual C# project types**.

4. Select **New project**. Under **Office** select **2007** and select **InfoPath 2007 Form** template and name the project as per your requirements.

5. Add the **System.Data.dll** reference to the solution.

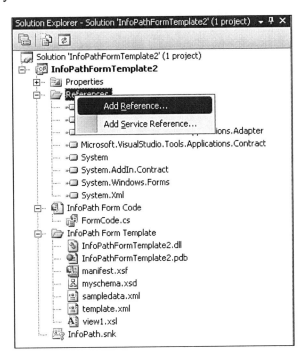

6. Add the following namespaces in the `formcode.cs` file:

```
using System.Data;
using System.Data.SqlClient;
```

7. The following code is used to connect to the Microsoft SQL Server database and populate the fields with data from the Microsoft SQL server:

```
public void FormEvents_Loading(object sender, LoadingEventArgs e)
{
// Initializing SqlConnection class.
    SqlConnection SQLDatabaseConnection = new SqlConnection();
// Passing ConnectionString property value to SqlConnection class
    SQLDatabaseConnection.ConnectionString = "Data Source=WINNER;
        Initial Catalog=PacktPub;Integrated Security=True";
    SQLDatabaseConnection.Open();
// Initializing SqlCommand class
    SqlCommand SQLDatabaseCommand = new SqlCommand();
// Passing the connection information
    SQLDatabaseCommand.Connection = SQLDatabaseConnection;
// Setting the command type
    SQLDatabaseCommand.CommandType = CommandType.Text;
// SQL Query
    SQLDatabaseCommand.CommandText = "select * from Books";
// Initializing SqlDataAdapter Class
    SqlDataAdapter SQLDatabaseDataAdapater = new
        SqlDataAdapter();
    SQLDatabaseDataAdapater.SelectCommand = SQLDatabaseCommand;
// Initializing DataSet Class
    DataSet SQLDatabaseDataSet = new DataSet();
    SQLDatabaseDataAdapater.Fill(SQLDatabaseDataSet);
// Reading data from dataset
    string strValue1 = SQLDatabaseDataSet.Tables[0].Rows[0][2].
        ToString();
    string strValue2 = SQLDatabaseDataSet.Tables[0].Rows[0][1].
        ToString();
// Assigning to the control
    XPathNavigator xNode1 = MainDataSource.CreateNavigator().
        SelectSingleNode("/my:myFields/my:field1",
        NamespaceManager);
    xNode1.SetValue(strValue1);
// Assigning to the control
    XPathNavigator xNode2 = MainDataSource.CreateNavigator().
        SelectSingleNode("/my:myFields/my:field2",
        NamespaceManager);
    xNode2.SetValue(strValue2);
}
```

In our example, the custom code to connect to Microsoft SQL Server and populating data in InfoPath fields is done from inside the form loading event. In this example, we connect to the database named `PacktPub` and get the data from the table named `Books`. The data retrieved from the database is shown to the user in the text box controls.

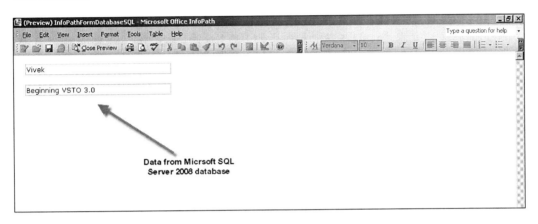

Working with Custom Task Panes

In Microsoft InfoPath, every control on a form must be bound to an element in the corresponding XML document. In turn, the contents of the XML document must be defined by a corresponding schema. These requirements can be limiting when you want to provide some added assistance to retrieve information and populate a form. These limitations are explained below.

Managed code

You can use managed code to display `System.Windows.Forms` dialog boxes that are launched by a button click on the form. But doing so comes at the cost of making development and deployment more complicated. For example, forms that you developed using Windows forms dialog boxes often cannot be deployed by a forms server.

Custom Task Pane

An alternative to managed code, in terms of supporting enterprise applications, is to use a **Custom Task Pane**. Microsoft Office 2007 supports custom task panes that provide you with tools to make available the features and the information your users or customers require at the place and time that they desire.

A Custom Task Pane in InfoPath 2007 is simply an HTML file that appears in the Task Pane (on the right-hand side of the InfoPath form). The HTML file can include form controls that are not bound to elements in the XML document. The HTML file can also have inline script, where the script can call back into the InfoPath object model, including calling any of your functions in the form code-behind script.

You can make web service calls from an HTML script, and you can also use InfoPath query adapters. InfoPath query adapters are used to retrieve data that is stored in the secondary data source (secondary data source is used to store data from supplementary or other data sources, as distinct from the current data source). We'll see how to do this in the next section.

 The Task Pane functions like a toolbar in such a way that you can move it around on the screen, dock the Task Pane horizontally or vertically, or separate it to keep it floating on the screen.

Creating an InfoPath Task Pane

To create an InfoPath Task Pane, follow the steps below:

1. Open Visual Studio 2008, and create a new **InfoPath 2007 Add-in** project.

2. In the Visual Studio solution, right-click on the reference and then click **Add Reference** on the **.NET** tab.

3. Scroll down to **Microsoft.Office.Interop.InfoPath.Xml**, and either double-click on it, or select it and then click on **OK**.

4. To add the user control for the Custom Task Pane, right-click the project, and then select **Add New Item** from the context menu. The **Add New Item** window is displayed; select **User Control**, name the user control **CustomTaskPane.cs** and click on **Add**.

5. In the Custom Task Pane, we are going to implement the number-to-word conversion concept and add the labels, textbox entries, and buttons required to build the user interface for the number-to-word converter functionality.

6. After building the user interface, the user control appears as shown in the following screenshot:

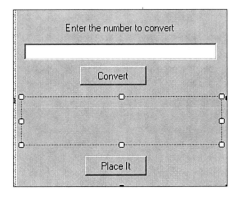

7. Add a global variable for your Task Pane immediately after the partial class declaration:

```
private CustomTaskPane CustomTaskPane;
```

8. Add a `Click` event for the button in the toolbar to open the Task Pane. You have to write the following code to call your Task Pane in this event handler.

```
private void openTaskPane_Click(Office._CommandBarButton src,
    ref bool Cancel)
{
// Task Pane Class initiation
    CustomTaskPane = new CustomTaskPane();
// Adding the Task Pane
    CustomTaskPanes.Add(CustomTaskPane, "Task Pane");
// Make the Task Pane to be visible for the users
    CustomTaskPanes[0].Visible = true;
}
```

9. Here is the code to append the custom button for our Task Pane into Microsoft InfoPath 2007. When the user clicks on this button, the Task Pane will be visible to the user.

```
private void ThisAddIn_Startup(object sender,
    System.EventArgs e)
{
  // Code to append the custom button we created to the
      standard toolbar
    if (this.Application.ActiveWindow != null)
    {
        Office.CommandBars AddInCommandBars = (Office.
            CommandBars)this.Application.ActiveWindow.CommandBars;
        Office.CommandBar AddInStandardBar =
            AddInCommandBars["Standard"];
```

```
    if (AddInStandardBar != null)
    {
        Office.CommandBarButton AddInConverterButton = (Office.
           CommandBarButton)AddInStandardBar.Controls.Add(
        Office.MsoControlType.msoControlButton, Type.Missing,
           Type.Missing, Type.Missing, true);
// Button properties
        AddInConverterButton.Caption = "CustomTask Pane";
        AddInConverterButton.Visible = true;
        AddInConverterButton.Enabled = true;
        AddInConverterButton.Style = Office.MsoButtonStyle.
           msoButtonCaption;
        AddInConverterButton.Click += new
           Office._CommandBarButtonEvents_ClickEventHandler(
           openTaskPane_Click);
    }
  }
}
```

10. Now, when you run the Visual Studio solution with InfoPath 2007, you can preview the InfoPath form template, as shown in the following screenshot.

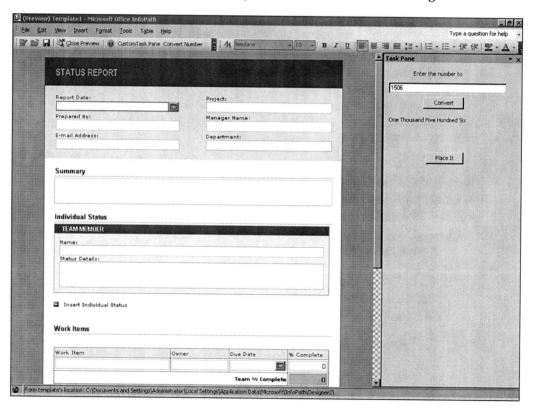

Writing InfoPath add-ins

Microsoft Office InfoPath 2007 provides a variety of features and flexibility for Office developers who want to enhance or customize InfoPath forms. Among these options is the ability to use Microsoft Visual Studio 2008 and VSTO to create an InfoPath 2007 application-level add-in. This means that, by using the Microsoft Office InfoPath 2007 object model, you can create add-ins for InfoPath 2007. So, in this section, we'll see how to create InfoPath add-ins using VSTO and Visual Studio 2008. InfoPath add-in is an option to add functionality to your InfoPath that is not available by default. Creating your own custom controls is just one way of extending the basic set of features included in InfoPath. By using COM add-ins, you can provide functionality that is not included in the core InfoPath application.

Creating an InfoPath add-in project using Visual Studio 2008

In this section, we'll see a step-by-step procedure for creating an InfoPath add-in. Although we'll create a specific add-in with this example, you can follow the same basic steps to create your own add-ins.

1. Start Microsoft Visual Studio 2008.

2. On the **File** menu, click on **New Project**.

3. In the **New Project** dialog box, expand **Visual C# project types**.

4.   Expand **Office project types**, and then select **2007**, as shown in following screenshot:

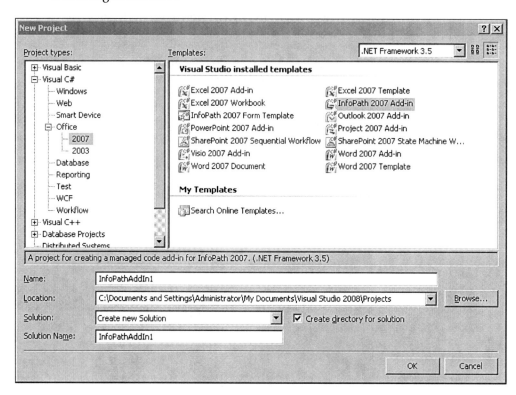

5.   In the **Templates** pane, select **InfoPath 2007 Add-in**. Enter any desired name in the **Name** box, and then click on **OK**. Now the solution for the **InfoPath 2007 Add-In** has been created successfully, as shown in the following screenshot:

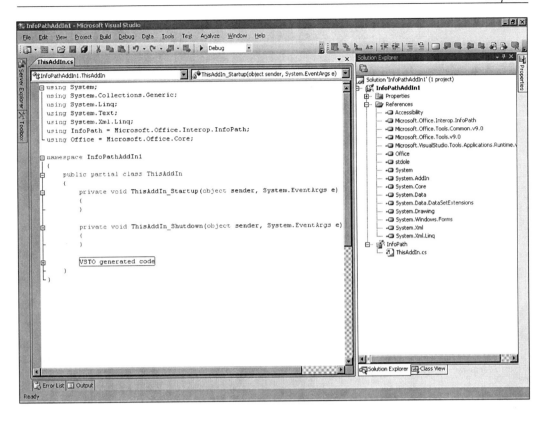

6. Right-click on the InfoPath add-in project solution, and select
   Add | Windows Form from the shortcut menu.

7. Name the form that you are adding to your InfoPath add-in solution.

8. Right-click on the InfoPath add-in project solution, and select
   Add | Class File from the shortcut menu.

9. Name the file **NumericConvertor.cs**.

10. Add Labels, Textbox, and Button controls to the windows form to create the user interface for your number-to-word convertor. Number-to-word converter is an example that has been included in this section to explain the add-in. It converts the numbers (stored as digits) into words; this functionality is not available in the InfoPath by default. The number-to-word conversion code has been written inside the NumericConvertor.cs, which is called for execution in the Windows forms added to your project. It appears as shown in the following image:

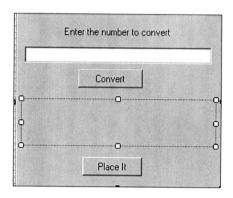

11. Here's the code to append the custom button for our add-in to Microsoft InfoPath 2007.

```
private void ThisAddIn_Startup(object sender, System.EventArgs e)
{
// Code to append the custom button we created to the standard
    toolbar
    if (this.Application.ActiveWindow != null)
    {
        Office.CommandBars AddInCommandBars = (Office.
            CommandBars)this.Application.ActiveWindow.CommandBars;
        Office.CommandBar AddInStandardBar =
            AddInCommandBars["Standard"];
        if (AddInStandardBar != null)
        {
          Office.CommandBarButton AddInConverterButton = (Office.
            CommandBarButton)AddInStandardBar.Controls.Add(
          Office.MsoControlType.msoControlButton, Type.Missing,
            Type.Missing, Type.Missing, true);
        // Button properties
          AddInConverterButton.Caption = "Convert Number";
          AddInConverterButton.Visible = true;
          AddInConverterButton.Enabled = true;
```

```
        AddInConverterButton.Style = Office.MsoButtonStyle.
            msoButtonCaption;

        AddInConverterButton.Click += new
            Office._CommandBarButtonEvents_ClickEventHandler(
            openAddIn_Click);
        }
    }
}
// Click event for the button in tool bar
private void openAddIn_Click(Office._CommandBarButton src,
        ref bool Cancel)
{
    InfoPathAddIn NumberConverter = new InfoPathAddIn();
// This will call the NumberConverter Add-In and it will be
        shown to the User
    NumberConverter.Show();
}
```

The number-to-word converter add-in will be visible in the Microsoft Office InfoPath 2007, and will appear as shown in the following screenshot.

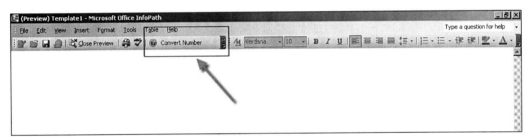

The number-to-word converter user interface appears as shown in the following screenshot.

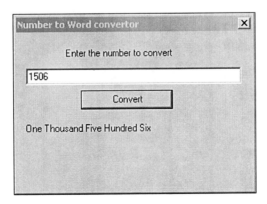

Let's continue the process and test the new functionality. Test the add-in by pressing F5. Visual Studio will compile the project and launch InfoPath. The form opens in Design mode, and you have no add-in. Click the **Preview** button.

You should see the **Convert** button on the far right side of the toolbar. The functionality for the number-to-word conversion is written in the `NumericConvertor.cs` file. But if you create your own add-in, the visual result will depend upon the core requirements of your project.

InfoPath and SharePoint workflow

Microsoft has created an innovative product that can be used to satisfy most enterprise collaboration needs. The solution is called **Microsoft SharePoint**, and is a comprehensive document management system. Microsoft SharePoint is a web-based document management system that has a variety of features and functionalities that can enhance your collaboration style and improve your business values. The term, SharePoint is commonly used to refer to Microsoft's two products Windows SharePoint Services and Microsoft Office SharePoint Server. Windows SharePoint Services 3.0 takes full advantage of Microsoft ASP.NET and the core Microsoft .NET runtime.

Microsoft Office InfoPath is one of the most useful Microsoft Office tools when combined with Microsoft SharePoint. Microsoft Office InfoPath has the ability to publish InfoPath forms on a SharePoint web site. This in turn allows InfoPath forms to be accessed from Internet Explorer, Firefox, Netscape, Safari, or mobile devices using **Form Services**. Microsoft Office InfoPath is well integrated with Office Server products such as SharePoint, so that you can build a **Workflow** solution for your business needs. For most activities for creating InfoPath forms, it is much easier to use InfoPath than designing ASPX pages. InfoPath forms also provide new capabilities, such as built-in data validation.

The Microsoft Windows Workflow Foundation is built on a .NET Framework. This is packaged with the .NET Framework 3.0 and the .NET Framework 3.5. It enables developers to create workflow-enabled applications. There are four main parts to Windows workflow:

- Workflow designer
- Activity model
- Workflow runtime
- Rules engine

Workflow in InfoPath can be used to implement role-specific form actions, role-based user features such as enabling forms, submitting emails, submitting to SharePoint based on certain rules, and so on.

The InfoPath form library is the primary integration point between Windows SharePoint Services and InfoPath. Microsoft InfoPath Forms Services is a server technology built on Microsoft Windows SharePoint Services 3.0 as an ASP.NET 2.0 application. The user experience of filling out a form in a browser is similar to that of filling out a form in InfoPath, but the purpose of this technology is to allow the user to run an InfoPath form inside the browser. An important goal is to reduce licensing costs for the customer and to increase business value.

Summary

This chapter has provided a complete view of Microsoft InfoPath 2007, and how it can be enhanced using VSTO 3.0. This chapter highlighted the capabilities of VSTO 3.0 and Visual Studio 2008. Along the way, we saw the essentials of VSTO and the InfoPath 2007 object model. By working with code in your InfoPath forms, we've seen how you can perform data source manipulation. We have also seen how you can use a custom Task Pane and InfoPath add-ins using the InfoPath 2007 object model. The bottom line is that Visual Studio 2008 has made the InfoPath 2007 programming environment easier and faster to use.

3
Microsoft Office Word Programming

Microsoft Office Word is the word processing software application released by Microsoft Corporation in the1980s for Xenix Systems. Later, Microsoft launched Word for the different platforms available in the market. Microsoft Office Word is part of the Microsoft Office Tools package. Microsoft Office Word is one of the most influential and comprehensive tools in the complete Microsoft Office software package. Even though Microsoft Office Word is now packed with several features and built-in functionality, the out-of-the-box Word features have never met the real world needs of business requirements. Windows form controls and business functionalities such as application-level solutions were unavailable until VSTO 2008, and could only be programmed only with VB6 or C++ as shared add-ins using plain COM technology.

Microsoft has finally given enough control and support in VSTO 2008, to enhance and add functionality to Microsoft Office Word using .NET technology. VSTO ships with a full set of managed APIs, which makes Word a normal programming experience for .NET developers. Automating the creation of data-rich business documents with Microsoft Office Word 2007 can be achieved with VSTO 3.0 and Visual Studio 2008.

In this chapter, we'll discuss:

- Word 2007 in Visual Studio, including how to create a Word solution in Visual Studio 2008
- Word solution—the object model and the object model functional area
- Document-level and application-level solutions
- Working with a Task Pane and creating custom Task Panes
- The concept of an Action Pane and managing Action Panes

- Host items and host controls
- Working with menus, toolbars and Ribbons
- Data binding concepts in Word 2007

Using VSTO 3.0, we can develop Word 2007 solutions at two levels: at the document level and at the application level.

For example, Microsoft Office Word 2007 automation is a great mechanism for populating business documents (including invoices, estimates, and reports) with data from backend systems. This type of repetitive task is typically performed by salaried office workers. Using VSTO 2008 Microsoft Office Word and VSTO 3.0, you can automate much of this routine work—making your workers available for more important work.

We can automate the creation of data-rich business documents with Microsoft Office Word 2007 using VSTO 3.0 and Visual Studio 2008. With automation and support for VSTO, Microsoft Office Word 2007 is more programmable than ever before. VSTO is the latest set of tools for programming Word.

Microsoft Office Word 2007 solutions

In older versions of Word, such as Microsoft Office 97, only macros could be used to enhance or automate a Word document. A macro is a series of commands that can be edited using Visual Basic Editor or by writing a VB6 or C++ unmanaged add-in.

For instance, a Word 2003 macro can be used to format an entire document with the same font and style. Macros are limited to scripting languages; new commands and behaviors cannot be built using macros.

Microsoft finally transcended macros following the introduction of Office 2003 with .NET platform support. For the first time, programmers were allowed to program Word and other Office applications using .NET languages, including C# and VB.NET. In VSTO 2008, VSTO's support for .NET programming languages finally moves us fully beyond the limitations of macros. Let's take a look at what these two levels mean.

Application-level solutions versus document-level solutions

VSTO 3.0 supports the creation of document-level solutions for Word, InfoPath, and Excel. Document-level solutions provide a document pointing to very specific tasks. The document-oriented approach can be used with documents in a uniform template that needs to be managed inside a team or company without affecting the application of the document that it resides in. For instance, a service business may wish to automatically generate invoices based upon customer data pulled from an SQL database.

An application object represents the whole application, whereas the document object represents the single document. With the document object, a specific type of document— in this example a programmatically created and filled-out invoice, is required; no changes to the application are necessary.

VSTO 3.0 is capable of having an application-oriented approach for all of the applications in the Office 2007 suite. You can implement a wide range of functionalities and features to your Office application through add-ins.

The ability to create application-level solutions using .NET technology is one of the key functionalities provided by the VSTO 3.0 for Office 2007 development. An application-level solution is customization done specifically to suit the application— in this case, Word 2007— and is available for all of the documents used by this application. The Task Pane customization and Ribbon customization are examples of application-level solutions that can be performed using VSTO. These concepts are explained in detail later in this chapter. A Task Pane button that generates our service business' invoice would appear in all instances of Word and would create a new behavior for the Word application.

Creating document-level solutions

In this section, you're going to see a simple document-level customized solution saying **Hello world**. This customization is specific to the document you've customized; the **Hello world** message appears whenever the document is opened. So every time you open this document, it displays the message. Even if you send the same document to other users, and the user opens the same document on a different machine running a different installation of Word 2007, the same message will be displayed. This is because the solution is document-level, and it resides in the document; the document being moved to a different location will not affect the solution. If a new instance of Word 2007 is started with a blank document, the text is not inserted.

Let's create a Word 2007 document solution using Visual Studio 2008. You will learn how the `Startup` and `Shutdown` events are used in the Word 2007 document solution. The `Startup` event is raised after the document is run and the `Shutdown` event is raised for each one of the documents, when the application domain, that the code is loaded in, is about to unload.

1. Open Visual Studio 2008, to create a new **Word 2007 Document** template project.

2. Select **New project**. Under **Office** select **2007** and here select **Word 2007 Document** and name the project according to your requirements. The following image shows the Visual Studio 2008 project template dialog box:

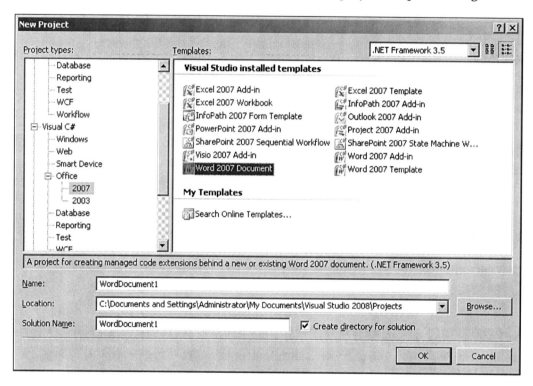

3. Next, you need to select the document type and name the document for your solution:

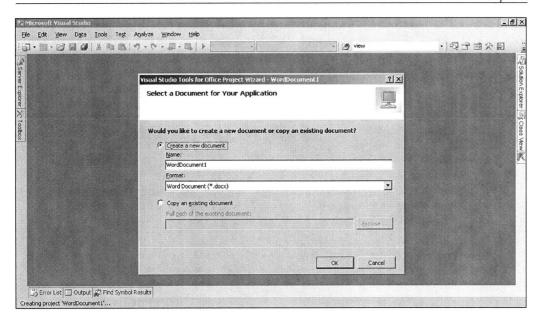

4. The solution will be created with all of the supporting files for the development of our Word solution. The newly-created Word 2007 document solution is displayed in the following image:

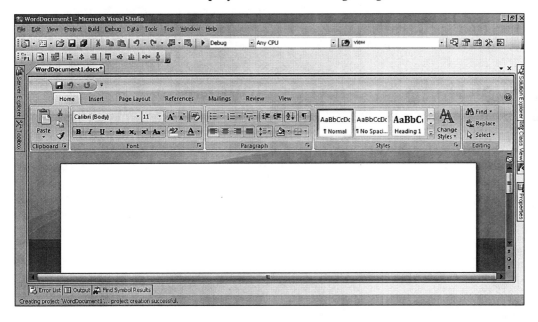

5. Write the program to customize the document in Microsoft Office Word 2007 inside the `ThisDocument.cs` file.

We'll set up this solution to run upon startup and shutdown of Microsoft Office Word 2007, using .NET programming. The `ThisDocument.cs` is the file where we will be writing our business logic, or the customization code for our Word solution, that you develop.

```
// Startup event for word application. Note the method signature
below—we'll see this alot.
// The Objects parameter indicates the sender and the event to be
received.
private void ThisDocument_Startup(object sender, System.EventArgs e)
{
    // We'll call a standard message box to show the text message to
        the document users
        MessageBox.Show("Welcome to Word 2007 Programming");
}

//Shutdown event for word application
private void ThisDocument_Shutdown(object sender, System.EventArgs e)
{
    // During document shutdown, we'll show a message to the users.
    // This is to show that you can do some operations during
        document shutdown.
        MessageBox.Show("Let's go back and explore more");
}
```

When making the move to Word 2007, dump everything you know about the **UI (User Interface)**. Everything has changed. You now have full freedom and control to create modern solutions in Word 2007 using VSTO with Visual Studio 2008.

Publishing solution deployment

The **ClickOnce** deployment technology allows Windows-based applications to be deployed and run with minimal user interaction. ClickOnce refers to an application deployment and maintenance procedure in which you compile your solution and publish it to a location available to your users. ClickOnce-deployed applications show lower consumption of resources — they are installed per-user, not per-machine. No administrator constitutional rights are required to install any of these applications.

Each ClickOnce application is isolated from the other, so that they do not affect other applications. You have a wide range of options to configure solution deployment manually or even automatically using wizards. Let's see the publishing of the process for custom Office application using these options.

Deployment using **Publish Wizard** automates the tasks of specifying the deployment settings. The wizard asks you to enter the path of the publishing folder and the installation folder.

1. Open Visual Studio 2008. From the menu select **Build | Publish WordDocument1**.

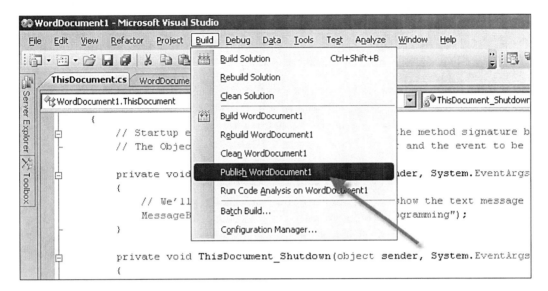

2. In the **Publish Wizard** dialog box, enter the location for the deployment files to be published, and then click **Next**.

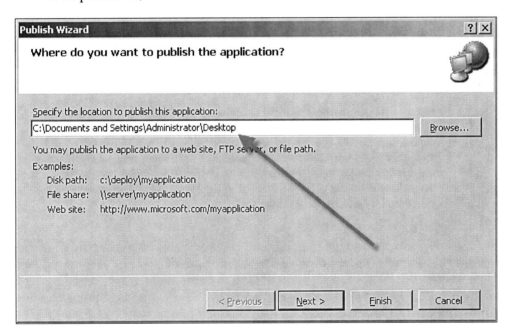

3. In the next step of the **Publish Wizard**, select **From a CD-ROM or DVD-ROM**. By specifying CD-ROM or DVD-ROM, you're telling the publishing wizard that the installation path is the same as the publish path. Click **Next**.

4. The **Publish Wizard** displays the publish location and declares itself ready to publish. Click **Finish** to publish the solution.

After you complete these steps, you can run the sample solution by opening the `WordDocument1.docx` file. When it opens, you should be able to see the customization that you have done in the document.

Working with objects and documents

As we get more efficient at developing solutions that use Microsoft Office Word, we can interact with the objects provided by the Word 2007 object model's huge number of methods, properties, objects, and events. Remember, an **object model** is a framework for developing and supporting program component objects that provide the underlying services of interface cooperation, life cycle management, and event services.

The most important aspect of developing and automating Office applications is to understand the object and the object model. Specifically, we have to look at how the objects and the object model works. Before we move onto application-level solutions, let's look at some basic Word 2007 objects. IntelliSense is Microsoft's implementation of auto-completion in Visual Studio's IDE. This will help the developer to easily access the objects, properties, and methods when programming.

When developing application-level solutions in Office 2007, you may need to access the objects of the application at the application-level for customization. If so, go ahead and create the project using the **Word 2007 Add-in Project** template, which is available in Visual Studio 2008. If the requirement is just to access the objects at document-level, then all you need to do is to create the project using the **Word 2007 Document Project** template available in Visual Studio 2008.

Word 2007 objects are arranged in a hierarchical order, and the two main classes at the top of the hierarchy are the application and document classes. An application object represents the whole application while a document object represents a single document. VSTO 3.0 extends several of these native objects into host items and host controls that can be used in document-level customizations.

For developing and automating Word 2007 solutions, we have to interact with and program objects that are provided by the Word object model. The Word object model can be accessed through the following main objects:

- `Application` object
- `Document` object
- `Range` object
- `Selection` object
- `Tables collection` object

Application object

The `Application` object represents the Word 2007 application, and is the parent of all of the other objects. You can use the `Application` object's properties and methods to manage the Word 2007 environment.

```
// To access the Application object
// Here 'methodname' represents the method available in the
   application object.
   this.Application.methodname
```

There is a lot of overlap in the Word 2007 object model. The overlap exists because there are multiple ways in which we can access the same type of object.

Document object

The `Document` object is one of the members of the `Application` object and is also a member of the `Selection` object. This is one area where an overlap occurs in the Word 2007 object model. By using the `Document` object you can manage independent documents separately in the Word 2007 solution.

```
// One of the ways to access Document object
// Here 'methodname' represents the method available in the
   application object.
   this.Application.Documents.methodname
```

Range object

The `Range` object is the object that you would use when you want to work with a range of spaces, borders, and so on, in Microsoft Office Word 2007. The `Range` object represents a bordering area in a document. It includes non-printing characters such as spaces, tab characters, and paragraph marks.

```
// One of the ways to access Range object
// Here 'methodorobjectname' represents the method available in the
   application object
   this.Application.ActiveDocument.Range.methodorobjectname
```

Selection object

The `Selection` object either represents the currently-selected area in our document, or it represents the insertion point, if nothing in the document is currently selected. If the requirement is to work with the active selection, you have to use the `Selection` object. This shares many properties and methods with the `Range` object.

```
// A few ways to access the Selection object
// Access the Selection object through ActiveDocument object
    this.Application.ActiveDocument.Sections;
// Access the Selection object through ActiveWindow object
    this.Application.ActiveWindow.Selection;
```

Tables collection object

The Tables collection is a collection of `Table` objects that represent the tables in a selection, range, or document. It is accessed via the construct `Tables (Index)`, where `Index` is the index number, which returns a single `Table` object. The index number represents the position of the table in the selection, range, or document.

```
// Way to access Table Object
    this.Application.ActiveDocument.Tables[int IndexValue];
```

Working with key objects

Now that you've seen a simple **Hello world** application and some basic methods, let's work out some of the underlying concepts of the Word 2007 object model, using some key objects in Word 2007. It is not feasible to entirely describe the Word object model in this section, but I'll try to make you comfortable with the most important objects in the Word object model and the most frequently used methods, properties, and events for these objects.

By using Word 2007, VSTO 3.0, and Visual Studio 2008, you can now apply sophisticated concepts including looping through collections, editing texts, working with range objects, prompting for information, and much more.

Inserting text in Word 2007 document

Inserting text in Word 2007 document can be achieved using `Range` objects and `Selection` objects. There are methods available for inserting text inside the Word 2007 document. `InsertAfter` method inserts text at the end of the active range or selection, whereas `InsertBefore` inserts text at the start of the active range or selection. The example code for both these methods is as follows:

```
// Using InsertBefore method inserts text
    this.Application.ActiveDocument.Content.InsertBefore("Text @ the
        Start - ");
// Using InsertAfter method inserts text

    this.Application.ActiveDocument.Content.InsertAfter(" - Text @
        the End");
```

The same insert text operation can be performed using the Selection object. The following is sample code for this:

```
// Using Selection Object inserting text after the text

    this.Application.Selection.InsertAfter(" - Text @ the End");
// Using Selection Object inserting text before the text

    this.Application.Selection.InsertBefore("Text @ the Start - ");
```

Selecting text in a Word 2007 document

Selecting text content in Word 2007 document can be achieved using the Sentences collection. By using the Range object, you can set the range of the text content to be selected in Word 2007. The Select() method is used to select text in Word 2007; this method is available in the Range object.

```
// Initializing the Range object
    Word.Range PacktRangeSelect;
// Check the sentence count
    if (this.Sentences.Count >= 1)
    {
// Set the start and ent point has object
        object pktStartFrom = this.Sentences[2].Start;
        object pktStopHere = this.Sentences[5].End;
// Assign the selection range
        PacktRangeSelect = this.Range(ref pktStartFrom,
            ref pktStopHere);
// Select the sentence using Select() method
        PacktRangeSelect.Select();
    }
    else
    {
        return;
    }
```

The following screenshot results after adding and executing the preceding code:

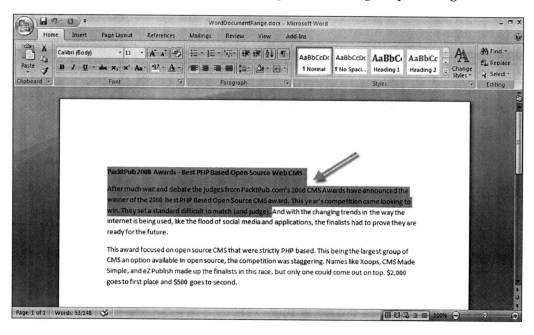

Creating a table in a Word 2007 document

Using the `Table` object we can programmatically create a table in Word. By using the `Range` object, you can set the range for the table to be drawn in Word 2007. We have a wide selection of options for setting the style property of the table that we are creating. In the following code sample, we are going to create a table with four columns and three rows:

```
// Object instance
// System.Type.Missing;Represents a missing value in the Type
   information. This field is read-only.
   object pktMissing = System.Type.Missing;
// Range on the application selection
   Word.Range PacktRangePresent = this.Application.Selection.Range;
// Using Table object add in the Word document
   Word.Table PacktTable = this.Application.ActiveDocument.Tables.
      Add(PacktRangePresent, 3, 4, ref pktMissing, ref pktMissing);
// Border propety of the Table we are creating
   Word.Border[] PacktBorder = new Word.Border[6];
   PacktBorder[0] = PacktTable.Borders[Word.WdBorderType.
                    wdBorderLeft];
   PacktBorder[1] = PacktTable.Borders[Word.WdBorderType.
                    wdBorderRight];
```

```
    PacktBorder[2]  = PacktTable.Borders[Word.WdBorderType.
                      wdBorderTop];
    PacktBorder[3]  = PacktTable.Borders[Word.WdBorderType.
                      wdBorderBottom];
    PacktBorder[4]  = PacktTable.Borders[Word.WdBorderType.
                      wdBorderHorizontal];
    PacktBorder[5]  = PacktTable.Borders[Word.WdBorderType.
                      wdBorderVertical];
// Border formatting of the Table
// Loop through the border and set color for table
    foreach (Word.Border pktBorder in PacktBorder)
    {
    // Table line style propety
        pktBorder.LineStyle = Word.WdLineStyle.wdLineStyleTriple;
    // Table line color property
        pktBorder.Color = Word.WdColor.wdColorGray30;
    }
```

A table with gray border gets created, as seen in the following screenshot:

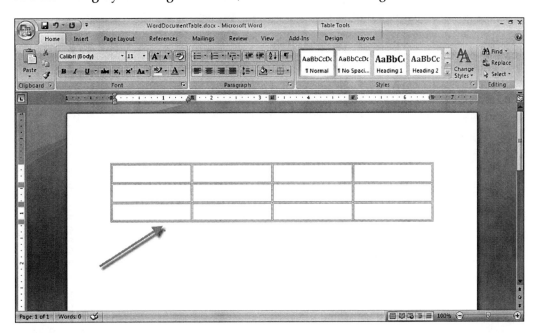

Working with Word templates

A **template** in Word 2007 is a re-usable format for a document. Microsoft Office Word 2007 templates contain sample content, formatting, and objects that can be used to quickly and easily create a new document. Word 2007 has a number of new key features such as content controls, targeted at developers, which will help you build more elegant and robust solutions.

Some of the key features include:

- **XML data**: Microsoft Office 2007 application provides wide support for XML format data widely. Microsoft Office InfoPath is a good example, in that its data is managed in the XML format.

- **XML mapping**: Microsoft Office 2007 features are mapped with XML. For example, the new Ribbon menu and the controls in the InfoPath are both mapped with the XML.

- **Content control**: Content controls are new controls that are used to manage data inside a Word document.

If you regularly create documents that contain a bunch of specific formatting, but not necessarily the same text, you can save yourself considerable time if you create Word templates to be used as the basis of future documents. Word templates can contain formatting, styles, headers, footers, and macros, in addition to dictionaries, toolbars, and autotext entries.

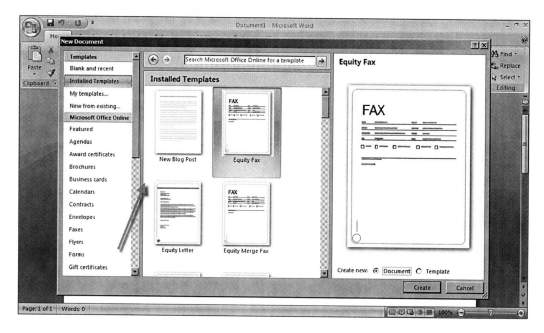

Microsoft Office Word 2007 has a wide variety of built-in templates for Office application users. The previous image represents the existing templates available in Microsoft Office Word 2007.

Actions Pane: Document-level customization

The Actions Pane is the customizable part of the document that is put together in a specific Microsoft Office Word 2007 document. Action Panes provide a convenient way for developers to introduce custom UIs into Office applications. Custom Actions Panes can be created and programmed using VSTO and Visual Studio 2008. You can program for events in the document to show and hide controls on the Actions Pane, and use HTML and CSS to create rich user interfaces inside a Word application in order to provide the user with an easily-accessible layout.

 The Custom Actions Pane is very different from the Custom Task Pane, even though they sound very similar. The Custom Task Pane is associated with application-level solutions, and the Custom Actions Pane is associated with document-level solutions.

Let's create a simple example of a Custom Actions Pane. Here, you are going to add a TextBox control to the Actions Pane and set the value for the TextBox property.

Creating a Custom Actions Pane for Microsoft Office Word 2007

The following steps will create a Custom Actions Pane for Microsoft Office Word 2007:

1. Open Visual Studio 2008 to create a new **Word 2007 Document** template project.

2. Select **New Project**. Under **Office**, select **2007** and then select the **Word 2007 Document** template and name the project as you wish.

3. Next, you need to select the document type, and name the document for your solution.

4. The solution will be created with all of the required supporting files for our development of the Word solution.

5. Write the following program to create a document in Microsoft Office Word 2007, inside the `ThisDocument.cs` file.

```
// Initializing the TextBox control to use in Actions Pane
    TextBox VSTOTextBox = new TextBox();

    private void ThisDocument_Startup(object sender,
        System.EventArgs e)
    {
        // Set the text property for the TextBox control
        VSTOTextBox.Text = "Say Hello to Actions Pane User";

        // Add the TextBox control to the ActionsPane
        ActionsPane.Controls.Add(VSTOTextBox);

        // On document load ActionsPane is shown
        ActionsPane.Show();
    }
```

6. The resulting Actions Pane is shown in the document pane, with the `TextBox` control added to Actions Pane. The following screenshot shows the Actions Pane in the document with added textbox control:

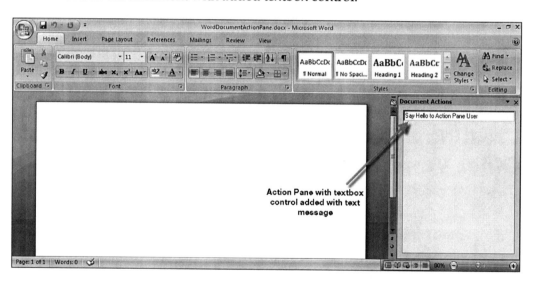

Action Pane with textbox control added with text message

Managing the Actions Pane

Actions Panes are not simply sliding windows that hold some controls and objects. Actions Panes consist of layers of containers. You can manage the position and size of each Actions Pane in Word 2007. You can even manipulate the controls present in an Actions Pane. Actions Panes support Windows form control to allow the design of custom Actions Panes.

The Actions Pane has several functions:

- It allows you to add a contextual user interface to the document.
- It provides you with the most flexible way of designing a custom user interface for the document.
- It takes care of user interface layout challenges, easily plugs into the Microsoft Office user interface, and acts like a dockable toolbar.
- It provides the ability to add Winform controls to the surface of a Word 2007 document. Winform controls are more flexible and interact with the Actions Pane through Visual C# .NET code, instead of HTML controls.

The `ActionsPane` object supports Windows form controls, and you can change the orientation of the Actions Pane programmatically.

The Actions Pane allows developers to host a Windows form control within the document's actions pane, which is more flexible for interacting with them through Visual C# .NET code when compared to HTML controls. The Actions Pane is built on top of the Task Pane object, and is composed of three objects: Actions Pane object, the Actions Pane controls, and Windows controls.

The following image represents the building blocks of the Actions Pane in Word 2007:

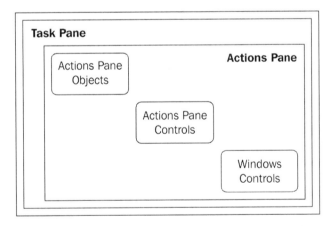

You can change the orientation of the Actions Pane. If the Actions Pane is docked vertically or horizontally, then this will have an impact on the stack order of the Actions Pane controls on the Actions Pane. VSTO 2008 provides access to the document Actions Pane via the new `ActionsPane` object.

Designing the Actions Pane

As we saw in the previous section, the Actions Pane is placed inside the document Actions Task pane, which is hosted within the Word Task pane. To customize the document Actions Task pane, you can use VSTO and Visual Studio's support for adding controls and creating rich user interfaces in the Actions Pane.

The DateTimePicker control will insert the selected date in a Word document. Let's add a DateTimePicker control to the Actions Pane:

1. Open Visual Studio 2008 to create a new **Word 2007 Document** template project.

2. Select **New Project**. Under **Office** select **2007** and then select the **Word 2007 Document** template, and name the project as you wish.

3. Next, you need to select the document type, and name the document for your solution.

4. The solution will be created with all of the required supporting files for our development of a Word solution.

5. Write the program to show Actions Pane in Microsoft Office Word 2007, inside the ThisDocument.cs file. You can add controls directly through the code. The following is the code snippet to add controls:

```
// Initializing the DateTimePicker control
  DateTimePicker _PacktDateTimePicker = new DateTimePicker();
// Code to add control in Document Actions Pane
  private void ThisDocument_Startup(object sender,
      System.EventArgs e)
  {
// Adding the DateTimePicker to the controls of the Actions Pane
      this.ActionsPane.Controls.Add(_PacktDateTimePicker);
  }
```

6. Next, to add the value selected from the DateTimePicker to the document content, you need to work on the events of the DateTimePicker control.

```
private void InternalStartup()
{
  // ValueChanged Event registration in the InternalStartup of
     the application
      this._PacktDateTimePicker.ValueChanged += new System.
         EventHandler(this._PacktDateTimePicker_ValueChanged);
}
// ValueChanged event of PacktDateTimePicker
private void PacktDateTimePicker_ValueChanged(object sender,
    EventArgs e)
{
```

```
        // Read content and insert the value after the paragraph
            this.Content.InsertParagraphAfter();
        // Insert value from the DateTimePicker select value
            this.Content.InsertAfter(PacktDateTimePicker.Value.
                ToString());
    }
```

Adding and executing the preceding code snippets, we get the following screenshot as an output:

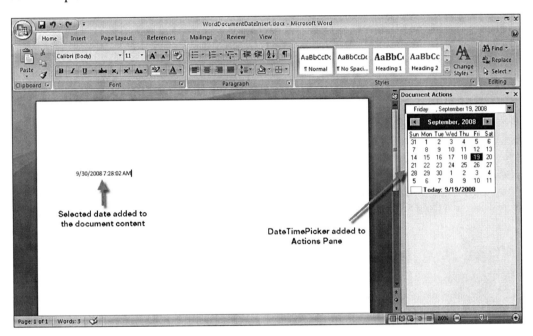

If you have a requirement to display a control on the Actions Pane in response to some events, then you can achieve the same by writing the code for any event available in Word 2007.

Application-level solutions

An application-level solution is one of the key functionalities provided by VSTO 3.0 for Office 2007 development using .NET technology. An application-level solution can be achieved by creating application-level add-ins. As we have mentioned earlier, the Task Pane customization and Ribbon customization are some of the application-level solutions that can be performed using VSTO. Whatever customization you do to the application will be in the Microsoft Office Word application, and this customization will be specific to the application that you are customizing, and it will be available for all of the documents used by this application.

Task Pane: Application-level customization

The Microsoft Office 2007 system provides a wealth of interface enhancements that make common tasks easier, and enhance user productivity. Microsoft has changed the way in which developers can create form-based solutions, by making Office 2007 development more consistent with development for other Microsoft Office products. In this section, we shall see how the Task Pane can be used to customize the user interface of Microsoft Office Word 2007 by using VSTO.

Normally, in Microsoft Office Word, to show some additional information or to gather user inputs from the user, it is necessary to use dialog boxes or forms. These forms and dialog boxes have several disadvantages. Forms don't provide programming language support for customization, and they appear inside the document content area. Dialog boxes appear as pop ups, and many users don't like this kind of interaction.

To overcome these disadvantages and deliver a rich user interface, Microsoft has come up with the Task Pane feature in Microsoft Office Word. Task Panes in Microsoft Office Word help you to get work done efficiently by bringing the tools you need right up close to your work. A Task Pane functions like a toolbar in that you can move it around on the screen, dock it horizontally or vertically, or detach it and keep it floating on the screen.

What is the Task Pane?

The Task Pane is one of the new features that have been included in Microsoft Office 2003/XP, and now in Microsoft Office 2007. The Microsoft Office system introduces custom task panes that give you the tools to provide the features and the information that your customers need.

A Microsoft Office 2007 Task Pane can contain one or more pages, and each page is broken up into sections. Microsoft Visual Studio Tools for the 2007 Microsoft Office system has opened up the Task Pane to developers in a new way. It enables developers to add Windows forms controls to the Task Pane, and interacts with the active document through the host's object model.

The Task Pane is a dockable dialog window, that appears on the rightmost side of the Microsoft Office Word application. You can also press the shortcut key *Shift* + *F7* to display the Search Task Pane. The Task Pane is context-sensitive, changing depending on the action. For instance, when you select **Custom Animation**, the Task Pane will change to show animation attributes and effects.

The Task Pane provides additional advantages for Office users and even Office developers. It provides a rich user interface, and hassle-free, quick access to the data required by users. Developers have the ability to customize a Task Pane through VSTO programming, and the ability to build a rich user interface using Windows forms controls.

Let's build a custom Task Pane. We'll start by simply building a Task Pane with a custom title.

1. Open Visual Studio 2008 to create a new **Word 2007 Add-In** template project.

2. Select a **New Project**. Under **Office** select **2007** then select the **Word 2007 Add-In** project template and name the project as you wish. The next image shows the Visual Studio 2008 project template dialog box.

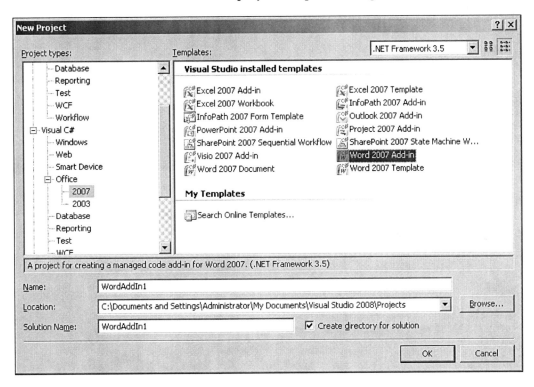

3. The solution will be created with all of the supporting files for our development of the Word solution. The next image shows the newly-created Word 2007 add-in solution.

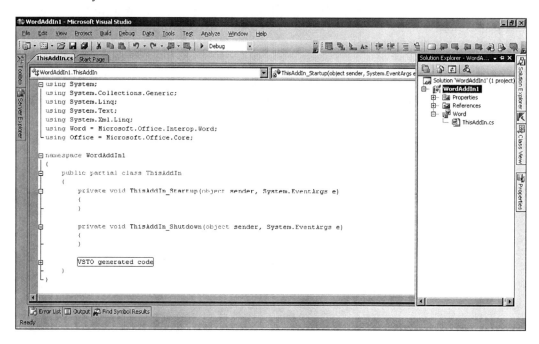

4. Write a program to show this Task Pane and a message on the startup of Word 2007, inside the `ThisAddIn.cs` file. This code will display a message in the title bar of the Task Pane of Word 2007.

```csharp
// Initializing the CustomTaskPane object of the current
   application
private Microsoft.Office.Tools.CustomTaskPane
    PacktTaskPaneControl = null;

// Iniatilizing the UserControl control
UserControl PacktUserControl = new UserControl();

// Loading the Task Pane on word start up
private void ThisAddIn_Startup(object sender, System.EventArgs e)
{
// Add the TextBox control to the CustomTaskPane
// The PacktUserControl parameter sets the title to "Sample
   Search"
    PacktTaskPaneControl = this.CustomTaskPanes.
        Add(PacktUserControl, "Sample Search");
// Set the CustomTaskPane to visible
    PacktTaskPaneControl.Visible = true;
}
```

Adding and executing the preceding code results in the following screenshot:

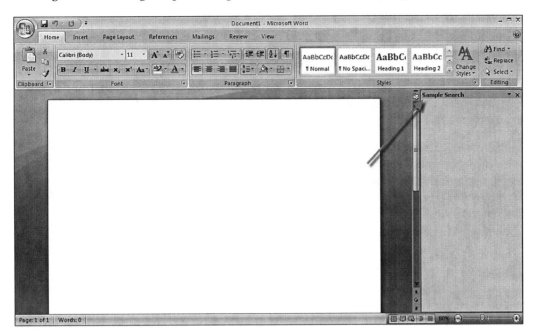

 While Task Panes can be customized as per user requirements and needs, Custom Task Panes give you a way to create your own Task Pane that provides users with a well-known interface to access your solution's features.

The Task Pane design also includes the three main design options:

- **Design templates** that include HTML layouts for Task Pane
- **Color schemes** that provide a way of creating a rich look and feel for Task Panes
- **Animation schemes** that let you do things such as adding animated files through the Windows Form control or through HTML elements

Microsoft Visual Studio Tools for the 2007 Microsoft Office system opened up the Task Pane to developers in a new way; it enabled developers to add Windows forms controls to the task pane and interact with the active document through the host's object model.

Custom Task Pane

Custom Task Panes give us a way to create our own Task Pane and provide Office users with a common interface to access our solution's features and functionalities. Users can customize the Task Pane in Microsoft Office Word 2007 application, and developers can customize Task Panes by programming in .NET using the Visual Studio 2008 IDE. In this section, we will learn how to program Custom Task Panes. Remember, as this is available to all Word 2007 users once installed, this is an application-level customization for Microsoft Office Word 2007.

Using Visual Studio IDE, we can create a multi-featured, integrated user interface with more interactive and easy-to-access features for Microsoft Office Word application users. We can create the Task Pane and bind its controls to the appropriate data sources, and make it interact with the host application. The Microsoft Office 2007 system applications do not include a built-in interface for showing and hiding your Custom Task Pane.

Creating a Custom Task Pane for Microsoft Office Word 2007

1. Open Visual Studio 2008 to create a new **Word 2007 Add-In** template project.
2. Select **New Project**. Under **Office**, select **2007** and the select the **Word 2007 Add-In** project template and name the project as you wish.
3. The solution will be created with all of the supporting files for our development of a Word solution.
4. Next, let's add the user control to be used in our Task Pane. Right-click on the project, and select **Add | User Control** from the context menu. Name the user control as **UserControl1.cs**, and click **OK**.
5. Now, in the Custom Task Pane, you are going to implement the calculator for Microsoft Office Word. Add the labels, textboxes, and buttons required to build the user interface for the calculator in the user control that you created in the previous step.

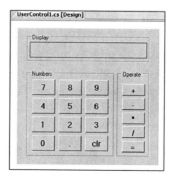

6. Write the program to display the Task Pane and the calculator in Microsoft Office Word 2007, inside the `ThisAddIn.cs` file. Let's show the calculator in the Task Pane of Word 2007.

```
// Initializing the CustomTaskPane object of the current
   application
private Microsoft.Office.Tools.CustomTaskPane
    PacktTaskPaneControl = null;

private void ThisAddIn_Startup(object sender, System.EventArgs e)
{
// Add the calculator Usercontrol to the TaskPane
    PacktTaskPaneControl = this.CustomTaskPanes.Add(new
        UserControl1(), "Calculator for Word");

// Make TaskPane visible
    PacktTaskPaneControl.Visible = true;

}
```

7. After building the user interface, the user control appears as shown in the following screenshot; the Custom Task Pane solution output shows the calculator.

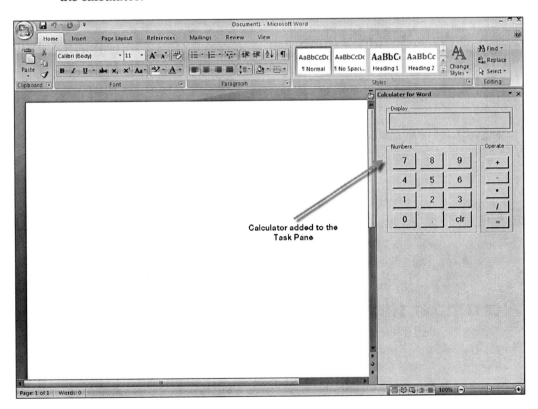

Calculator added to the Task Pane

Programming in Word

When programming in Microsoft Office Word 2007, the tools and techniques needed to program using C# for applications are VSTO 3.0, Visual Studio 2008, and the .NET framework. So far, we've learned that by using VSTO 3.0, we can program forms, controls, objects, and error handling, and have learned that VSTO 3.0 enables rapid application development for Microsoft Office solutions. VSTO 3.0 gives the Office developers the flexibility to create document-level customizations and application-level add-ins by using Visual C#, .NET, and Visual Studio 2008.

Microsoft has come up with a variety of Word 2007- supported objects that are exposed from the Office object model, allowing Office developers to program against the exposed objects for the development and customization of Word 2007. In general, while automating the Office applications using managed code, you program against the **primary interop Office assemblies**.

 A primary interop assembly is an exceptional, vendor-supplied assembly that includes type definitions. A single primary interop assembly can wrap more than one version of the same type of library.

In VSTO 3.0 solutions, you can write code against the host items in your VSTO projects. The following table provides an overview of the assembly reference changes in VSTO 3.0:

Before VSTO 3.0 full release	After VSTO 3.0 full release
ServerDocument.dll	ServerDocument.v9.0.dll
Microsoft.VisualStudio.Tools.Office.dll	Microsoft.Office.Tools.v9.0.dll
Microsoft.VisualStudio.Tools.Office.Common.dll	Microsoft.Office.Tools.Common.v9.0.dll
Microsoft.VisualStudio.Tools.Office.Word.dll	Microsoft.Office.Tools.Word.v9.0.dll

This quick overview will help VSTO 3.0 developers to understand how the new version differs from the previous version.

Word host items

Host items present a way in for our code in Visual Studio Tools for Office solutions. Host items and host controls are the two classes that provide us the programming models for the Visual Studio Tools for Office solution. This interacts well with Office COM components, just as object model interaction takes place.

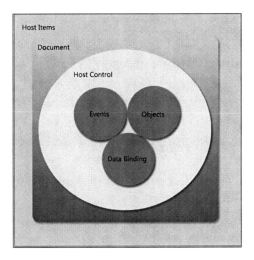

The preceding image gives us an overview of the Word 2007 host items and the host controls of the Word document. Each host item can host more than one host control for the document. Each and every host control will expose events, objects, and data binding properties for the Word 2007 customization.

Host items have a few programmatic limitations. At the document level, we can have only one host item. That is, we cannot add programmatically to the document. Also, document-level host items can be created only at design time. Host items have designers, which act as the visual representation of the classes. Host items act as the containers for the controls, such as host controls and Windows form controls. Host items provide a means for displaying data by Word document class.

Word host controls

VSTO 3.0 extends data binding to Office solutions by enabling programmers to bind data to objects such as bookmarks, ranges, and so on. These objects are called host controls; they are controls that apply to a given application. Host controls are based on native Office objects. Enriched host controls extend Office object models, offer great flexibility in data binding, and enhance event model features. Host controls are also called **Office-specific controls**.

Word host controls extend the host application (Word) object model to provide new functionality or to improve programmability. Word host controls are part of Word 2007 application customizations, and support both document-level and application-level customizations.

Let's see a sample program that will add bookmark controls to a Word 2007 document using bookmark host control.

1. Open Visual Studio 2008 to create a new **Word 2007 Document** template project.

2. Select **New Project**. Under **Office** select **2007** and then select the **Word 2007 Document** template and name the project.

3. Next, you need to select the document type, and name the document for your solution.

4. The solution will be created with all of the supporting files for our development of the Word solution.

5. Write the program to add a bookmark control in Microsoft Office Word 2007, inside the ThisDocument.cs file.

```
// Adding bookmark control to document at runtime
    private void ThisDocument_Startup(object sender,
        System.EventArgs e)
    {
      // Initializing the Bookmark object
        Microsoft.Office.Tools.Word.Bookmark PacktParagraph;

      // Add the bookmark range and set the text value
        PacktParagraph = this.Controls.AddBookmark(this.
            Paragraphs[1].Range, "First Paragraph");

      // Add the paragraph text entry
        PacktParagraph.Text = "Hello World";
    }
```

Adding controls to a document

Adding controls to a document can be achieved in design mode and also programmatically. Let's see how to add a control to the document solution created, at run-time, and in a simple and elegant way.

In this section, we'll add ActiveX to our VSTO Word 2007 document solution.

 ActiveX, in case you didn't know, is a component object model developed by Microsoft for the Windows platform. ActiveX controls are used for customized applications for gathering data, viewing different kinds of files, and so on.

Adding an ActiveX control to Microsoft Office Word 2007 programmatically

In this example, let's add an ActiveX calendar control to the document-level customization. In an earlier part of this book, you have seen an example with `DateTimePicker`. `DateTimePicker` is a Windows forms control, and the calendar control that you are using in this example is an ActiveX control. This is to demonstrate that ActiveX controls can be used for Office 2007 customization when customizing using VSTO.

1. Open Visual Studio 2008, create a new **Word 2007 Document** project, and name the solution as you desire.

2. Next, let's add the user control to be used for our solution. Right-click on the project, and select **Add | User Control**. Name the user control **UserControl1.cs** and click **OK**.

3. Next expand the Visual Studio **Toolbox**, right-click on the **Toolbox** and select **Choose Items** from the context menu.

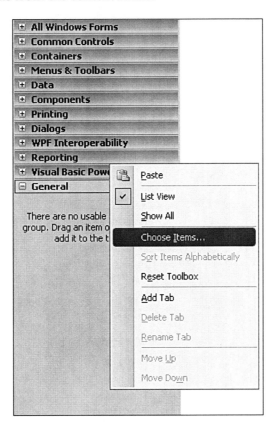

4. In the **Choose Toolbox Items** dialog box, select the **COM Components** tab, and then select the checkbox next to **Calendar Control 12.0**. This is a native ActiveX control in the **MSCAL.OCX** DLL file.

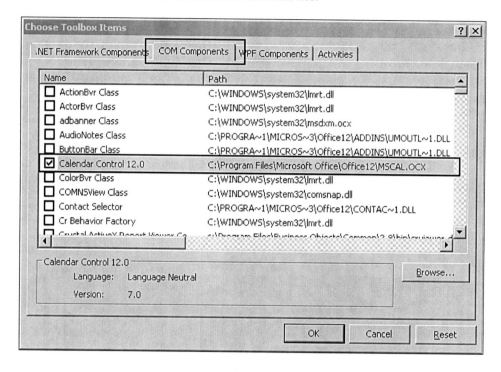

5. After adding the **Calendar Control 12.0** ActiveX control, you can see that the control has been added to your toolbox for Visual Studio 2008, as shown in the following screenshot:

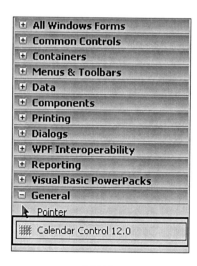

6. Now, a developer can drag-and-drop the ActiveX control into the **UserControl** that we will add to our Word 2007 document solution.

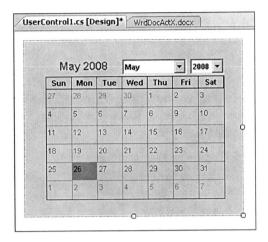

7. In the `ThisDocument` class, declare an instance of the `UserControl1` wrapper, with `UserControl1` as a private field in the class:

```
// Declare the instance of our UserControl
   private UserControl1 ManagedActiveXCtrl;
```

8. In the `ThisDocument_Startup` method, instantiate `UserControl1` and its `ClickEvent`, and add the control to the Actions Pane of our document. When the user clicks on the date in the calendar, write the selected date value in the Word work-space.

```
// StartUp method of our Document in the solution
   private void ThisDocument_Startup(object sender,
      System.EventArgs e)
   {
// Initializing the instance of the User control
   ManagedActiveXCtrl = new UserControl1();

// Register the click event of the control
   ManagedActiveXCtrl.axCalendar1.ClickEvent += new
      System.EventHandler(axCalendar1_ClickEvent);

// Add the control to the Actions Pane
   this.ActionsPane.Controls.Add(ManagedActiveXCtrl);
   }

// Click event of our User Control
   private void axCalendar1_ClickEvent(object sender,
      EventArgs e)
   {
```

```
        // Insert the selected date to the content
            this.Content.InsertParagraphAfter();

        // Insert the date after converted to string
            this.Content.InsertAfter(this.ManagedActiveXCtrl.
                axCalendar1.Value.ToString());
    }
```

9. We have successfully implemented a simple ActiveX control in the Word 2007 document solution through programming. Now, run the solution to see the result. It will be similar to the following image. Note that date is added in the current system date-time format.

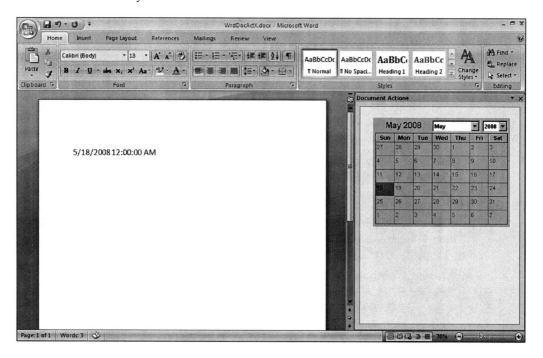

Data binding to host controls

In VSTO 3.0, data binding to the host controls is one of the features that improves Office 2007 programming. The new Visual Studio 2008 GUI data tools allow you to bind data from an SQL Server database to host controls and Windows form controls within your Visual Studio Tools for Office document.

Displaying XML data in XML Node host controls within a Word document is made easy with the new Visual Studio environment—by connecting to data sources using the data sources window or data access objects. First, let's have an architectural overview of Office 2007 data access objects.

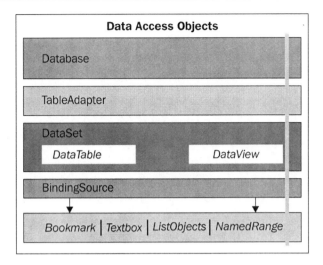

Data binding in Microsoft Office Word can be done in two ways:

- Simple data binding
- Complex data binding

Let's begin with simple data binding. In simple data binding, we'll bind data from Microsoft SQL Server 2008 to the Microsoft Office Word 2007. Later, you will learn the concept of complex data binding.

Simple data binding

In simple data binding, a control property is bound to a single data element. With the exception of the XMLNodes control, all host controls support simple data bindings.

Office Word 2007 has a new type of control called content controls. Content controls are containers within which specific types of content, such as dates, lists, pictures, or text, can be placed. Let's work out a simple data binding in Word 2007 using Visual Studio 2008:

1. Open Visual Studio 2008, to create a new **Word 2007 Document** template project.
2. Select **New Project**. Under **Office,** select **2007**. Then, select the **Word 2007 Document** template, and give the the project a name of your choice.
3. Next, you need to select the document type, and name the document for your solution.

4. The solution will be created with all of the supporting files necessary for the development of our Word solution.

5. Within the document, draw a table with two rows and four columns, as shown in the following screenshot:

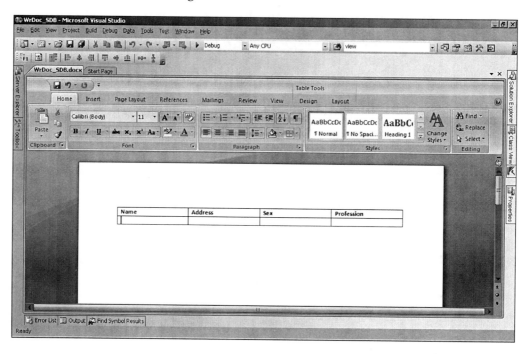

6. Next, we need to add a data source to our Word 2007 document solution. In Visual Studio 2008, under the **Data** menu select **Add New Data Source**.

7. The **Data Source Configuration** wizard will appear with **Database**, **Service**, and **Objects** as your **Data Source options**.

8. Select **Database**, and click the **Next** button to proceed.

9. Now, the wizard will take you to the **Choose Your Data Connection** screen. Click on the **New Connection** button to proceed.

10. On the **New Connection** screen, select the **Data Source** and **Data Provider**, and test the connection. As soon as the testing process has completed, the new connection information will be automatically added to your connection drop-down list.

11. Next, save the connection string to the application configuration file, enter the connection string that you want to appear in the application configuration file, and proceed by clicking **Next**.

12. To choose our database objects, refer to the following screenshot. In this example, you have selected the table that was created to display the profile information.

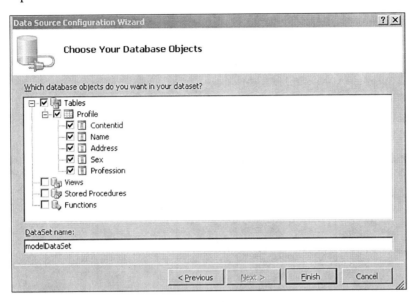

13. Click **Finish**. Now the Data Source created will appear in your Visual Studio 2008, as shown in the following screenshot:

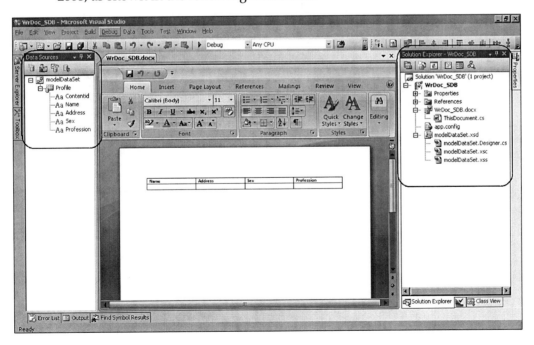

14. Depending upon the data items, the Data Source items will be mapped to the corresponding controls by default. These mappings can be changed to other controls later, as per our requirement. By default, all of the data items in our Data Source are mapped to `PlainTextContentControl`. Next, drag-and-drop the data item from the Data Source to the position in the document where you want it to be displayed.

15. Let's change the default control for our data items. In our example, we'll change the **Professional** data item from `PlainTextContentControl` to **Bookmark**. To do this, select the data item, and a drop-down menu with a button will appear on it. When you click on this button, you will see the list of controls that are available to be mapped to our data item.

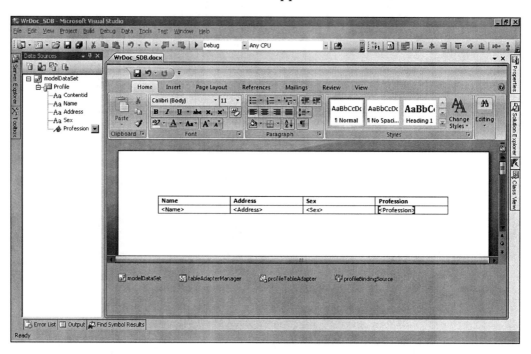

16. Run the solution to see the result. The first record in the database will be displayed in the table inside the document, as shown in the following screenshot:

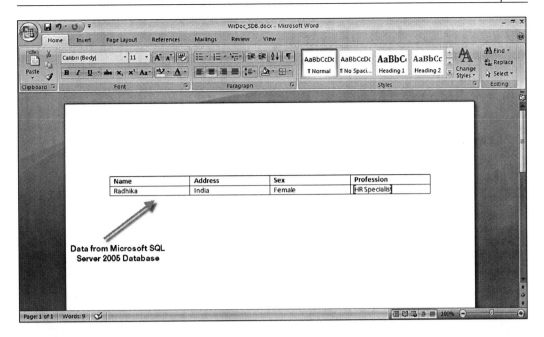

Data from Microsoft SQL
Server 2005 Database

You can perform these kinds of data manipulations by using .NET programming. Let's look at a simple example of data manipulation. Here, you will be protecting the data shown in the Word document by setting it to **locked,** by using custom code.

> Lock control is simply the process of setting the data to read-only, protecting it from editing by another user.

Change the data item **Contentid** to be a **Combobox** control, and place this control in the document. By using this drop-down box, we can jump to the data items that we want to view inside the document. We will place the procedure to lock or unlock the content control inside the `Enter` event of the content control.

Write a program to create a document in Microsoft Office Word 2007, in the `ThisDocument.cs` file.

Let's see the code snippet to lock or unlock the content control of our data item that is displayed in the document:

```
// Enter Event of Address Content Control
    private void ptAddressCtrl_Entering(object sender, Microsoft.
        Office.Tools.Word.ContentControlEnteringEventArgs e)
    {
      // Display the dialog window for the edit operation
        System.Windows.Forms.DialogResult myResult = new
```

```
                    DialogResult();
// Message with Yes/No option to proceed
    myResult = MessageBox.Show("Do you want to UnLock?",
        "Edit Address?", MessageBoxButtons.YesNo,
        MessageBoxIcon.Question, MessageBoxDefaultButton.
        Button2, MessageBoxOptions.DefaultDesktopOnly, false);
// If you select the no it will remain in lock mode and display
    the content
    if (myResult == DialogResult.Yes)
        ptAddressCtrl.LockContentControl = false;
}
```

The results of addition of this code, can be seen in the following screenshot:

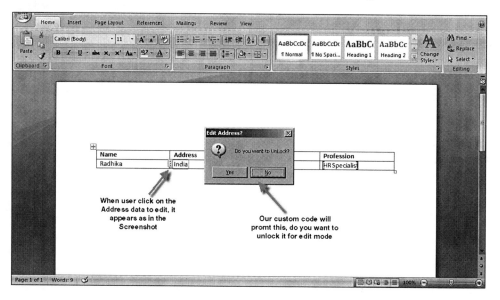

Complex data binding

In simple data binding, a single property of the control is bound to a single value in the data model, for example, binding a value to the TextBox controls text property. With complex data binding, you bind a control to a collection of data items. For example, a datagrid/dataview control binds to a dataset that is a collection of data items. This is the main difference between simple data binding and complex data binding.

Complex data binding works best with new data management concepts and technologies, and the most modern data management technology in .NET is **LINQ (Language Integrated Query)**. VSTO 3.0 supports LINQ for data management and manipulation for the development of Office application solutions.

What is LINQ?

LINQ is a programming model that introduces queries as a first-class concept into any Microsoft .NET language. LINQ is all about queries, whether they are queries returning a set of matching objects, a single object, or a subset of fields from an object or a set of objects. LINQ is one of the key features of the Microsoft .NET Framework 3.5.

LINQ queries can directly populate an object hierarchy, and parameterization is automatic and type-safe, which is more extensive in application development. In Visual Studio 2008, nearly all projects automatically include references to `System.Core` and `System.Xml.Linq`, where most of the LINQ classes are defined.

Using LINQ in Word 2007 with VSTO 3.0 and Visual Studio 2008

1. Open Visual Studio 2008, to create a new **Word 2007 Document** template project.
2. Select **New Project**. Under **Office**, select **2007** and then select the **Word 2007 Document** template, and name the project as you wish.
3. Next, you need to select the document type, and name the document for your solution.
4. The solution will be created with all of the supporting files required for the development of our Word solution.
5. In the `Startup` event of the Word document, let's do some string manipulation using LINQ.
6. In this simple demonstration, you are going to see how to query a string and retrieve the number of words in the string. This is going to be achieved by using LINQ and lambda expressions. A **lambda** expression is an unspecified function that can contain expressions and statements, and all lambda expressions use the lambda operator (=>), which is read as "goes to".

```
private void ThisDocument_Startup(object sender, System.EventArgs
{
  // String to store the title text
    String strText = "Beginning VSTO from PacktPub";

  // Use LINQ and implicit types to get the word count
    var qChars = from c in strText select c;
    int charCount = qChars.Count();

  // Use lambda expression to get the number of words.
    List<string> textWords = new List<string>(strText.
        Split(new char[] { ' ' }));
```

```
    var qLetterWords = textWords.FindAll(x => (x.Length >= 2));
// Insert in the word using selection objects
    this.Application.Selection.InsertAfter("\n Character Count:
        " + charCount + "\n Word Count: " + qLetterWords.Count);
}
```

7. Run the solution from Visual Studio, to insert the text into the Word document, as shown in the following screenshot:

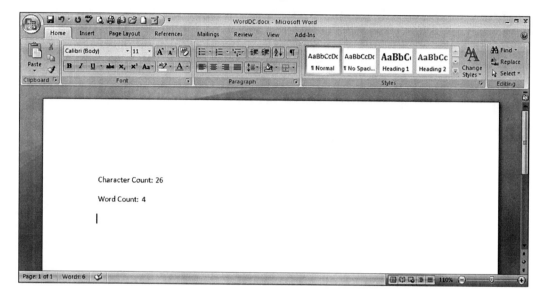

Complex data binding works with new data management concepts and technologies. VSTO 3.0 also supports LINQ for data management and manipulation for the development of Office application solution. In the above demonstration for complex data binding, using LINQ in Word 2007 document solution provides you with a demonstration of how extensive VSTO 3.0 is, supporting the creation of Office applications for every business need.

Customization

Microsoft Office Word 2007 is a powerful authoring tool that gives you the ability to create and share documents. Advanced integration with Microsoft Office SharePoint Server 2007 and new XML-based file formats make Microsoft Office Word 2007 the ideal choice for building integrated document management solutions, by providing users with an enterprise collaboration solution, managing the content and data in a centralized system. Microsoft Office Word 2007 helps information workers to create professional-looking content more quickly than ever before.

Microsoft Office Word 2007 has a variety of new features that help users to create and manage more specific documents for their needs. But Microsoft Office Word 2007 window can be confusing to users who are familiar with the previous versions of Microsoft Office Word. Apart from the new features and functionality, Microsoft Office 2007 has come up with customization options for most of the features, including the Quick Access Toolbar, Shortcut Keys, AutoCorrect, Status Bar, Menus, Watermark, Document themes, and the Ribbon.

To make life easier for your users, you can now extensively customize the Word 2007 interface. This customization can be achieved in two ways—first, through the Microsoft Office Word 2007 user interface tools (which can be done even by end-users) and, second, by programming in the .NET and VSTO platforms.

Ribbon menu

In Microsoft Office Word 2007, all of the, classic, menus have been replaced by a new style of menu called the Ribbon. Microsoft describes the Ribbon in the following way:

> *The Ribbon replaces the current system of layered menus, toolbars, and task panes with a simpler system of interfaces optimized for efficiency and discoverability.*

New users may find it a little harder to locate what they are looking for in the Ribbon menu, because they are new to this style of interface. If you have existing Word macros that use menus or toolbars, they will usually work in Office 2007; but the implementation is not attractive.

The previous image shows the default Ribbon menu options in Word 2007. Even though everyone seems to hate the Ribbon, there are many nice features. The Ribbon menu is more advantageous than the old menu because it brings all of the features of Office 2007 directly to the users. The Ribbon menu also brings a better visual representation to the user, in order to identify the menu that they are searching for. Although the Ribbon is larger than the old menu system, it doesn't seem to take anymore UI space in the Word document, as the new Ribbon effectively replaces the menu bar, floating palettes, and toolbars.

You don't have any out-of-the-box features to enable the classic menu style in Word 2007, but we can achieve the same classic menu item in the UI and almost 100% of the original functionality, by adding third-party add-in controls. Users can customize the Ribbon by using the built-in features available, with a few more limitations. We can customize, add control, and do more using the VSTO 3.0 runtime and .NET programming at the document-level and the application-level of Word 2007.

Adding controls to menus

Developers have complete control over customizing the Ribbon in Word 2007. The design around the Ribbon is fairly simple. It's a tabbed strip interface that contains a set of groups. Each of these groups can contain a number of controls, with each control potentially having a different type. These might be buttons, drop-down menus, textboxes, and so on. These controls can be grouped in a nested fashion within the definition, and the user interface will display it continuously.

Let's do some simple customization of the Ribbon menus in Microsoft Office Word 2007. Follow the steps given below to add controls and customize your Word 2007 menu.

1. Open Visual Studio 2008, to create a new **Word 2007 Add-In** template project.

2. Select **New Project**. Under **Office**, select **2007**, and then select the **Word 2007 Add-In** template, and give the project a name.

3. The solution will be created. Along with with all the supporting files required for the development of our Word solution.

4. Next, let's add the Ribbon component to our solution. Right-click on the project, and select **Add | New Item... | Ribbon (Visual Designer)** (A control that provides a visual designer for basic Ribbon customization tasks) from the context menu.

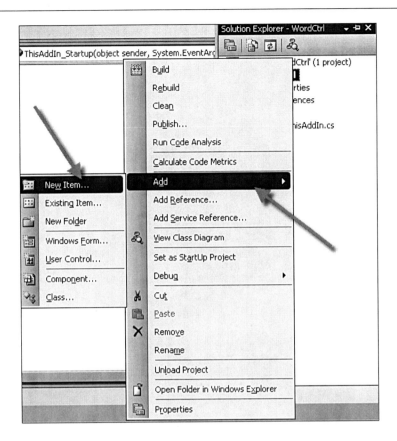

5. Name the Ribbon component **Ribbon1.cs**, and then click **OK**.

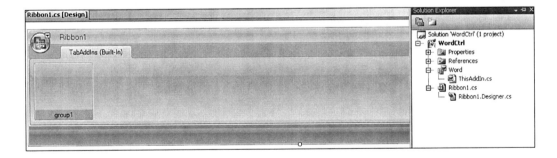

6. Expand the toolbox window in Visual Studio 2008, and you can find the controls that support the Ribbon menu in Office customization.

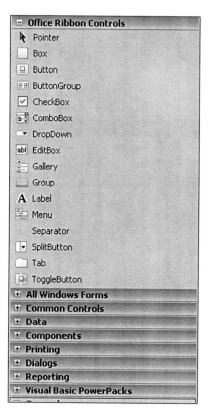

7. Drag-and-drop the `ToggleButton` control that's required for the development, to inside your group control in the Ribbon.

8. Right-click on the control, and then select **Properties**. In the **Properties** window, select the **Click** event under **Events**. Following is the code for the **Click** event of the `ToggleButton` in the custom Ribbon.

```
// Click event of the ToggleButton
    private void toggleButton1_Click(object sender,
        RibbonControlEventArgs e)
    {
// Inserting text in the active window using Range Object
        Microsoft.Office.Interop.Word.Range rngWordRange =
            Globals.ThisAddIn.Application.Selection.Range;

// Set the text for the text properties
        rngWordRange.Text = "Microsoft - VSTO Book \n";
    }
```

9. Run the solution from Visual Studio to see the output of the solution.

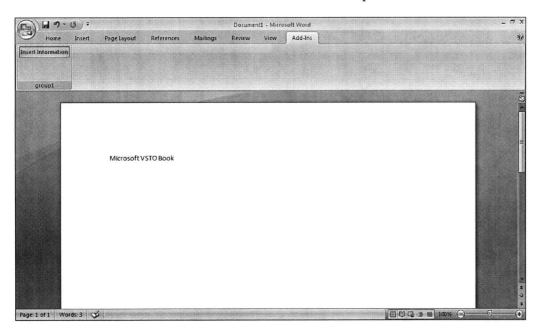

If there is a requirement to add or customize a Microsoft Office button (Office menu) in Word 2007, we can do so in VSTO 3.0. Repeat steps one to five of the previous operation, and then, follow these instructions:

1. Drag the button control and drop it inside the Office menu. The following images represent the two controls that have been added to the OfficeMenu item.

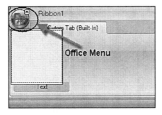

2. Next, add the following code to the event of the button control. This is placed in the `Ribbon1.cs` file of your solution

```
private void button1_Click(object sender,
    RibbonControlEventArgs e)
{
// Show a message box!
    System.Windows.Forms.MessageBox.Show("Menu Item in Word
        2007");
}
```

3. Run the solution from Visual Studio to see the output for the solution that is similar to the following screenshot:

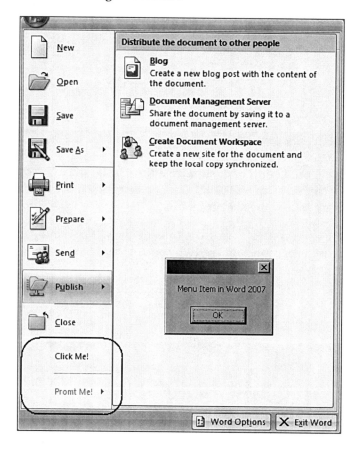

Toolbar (Quick Access Toolbar)

In earlier versions of Word, developers could customize the toolbars. We could even create our own custom toolbar by using custom coding. Even though the Ribbon is quicker and easier than the classic toolbars, you may find yourself wishing for certain commands that used to be immediately available on a toolbar and are now hidden somewhere within the Ribbon. To satisfy Word 2007 users' need for familiarity, and Word 2007 developers' desire to customize, Microsoft Office Word 2007 comes with the **Quick Access Toolbar (QAT)**, which can be customized to suit our needs. The following images represent the default view of the Quick Access Toolbar in Word 2007:

Adding controls to toolbars

Users have the option to add often-used commands, or commands missing from the Ribbon command buttons to the QAT. There are a few ways to do this. One option is to right-click on the command button on the Ribbon, and choose **Add to Quick Access Toolbar** from the shortcut menu (refer to the previous image.) You can also access the QAT through coding by using VSTO 3.0 and .NET programming.

Performing a range of actions on the 2007 Microsoft Office Fluent User Interface, such as customizing the Quick Access Toolbar, requires only a few lines of XML and programming code. The 2007 Microsoft Office Fluent UI replaces the current system of layered menus, toolbars, and Task Panes with a simpler system that is optimized for competence and discoverability. We can add components to the Office Fluent Ribbon by using XML markup elements, and we can set the properties of these components by using attributes. We can assign functionality to the components by using any programming language supported by Microsoft Visual Studio 2008, such as Microsoft Visual C#, and Microsoft Visual Basic.

From within VSTO 2008, there are two possible ways to customize the Office Fluent UI Quick Access Toolbar. One way is modify an Office Open XML format file created by one of the Microsoft Office applications that support the Office Fluent UI.

Another way is to use an add-in. The Office Fluent UI has been built by Microsoft so that XML is capable of providing a hierarchical and declarative model for the user interface. You add controls to QAT by using XML elements to indicate the type of component.

 Every Office developer must understand that when customizing the QAT, it has to be started from scratch. We must set the `startFromScratch` attribute to `true`:

```
<ribbon startFromScratch="true">
```

The XML markup for QAT document controls is provided here:

```
<customUI xmlns="http://schemas.microsoft.com/Office/2006/
    01/customui" onLoad="Ribbon_Load">
  <ribbon>
    <qat>
      <sharedControls>
        <button idMso="Copy" />
        <button idMso="Paste" />
      </sharedControls>
    </qat>
  </ribbon>
</customUI>
```

The following table provides a quick overview of the child elements of the Quick Access Toolbar in Office 2007:

Objects	Need for the Object
control	Generic control object that can represent other objects such as a button, splitButton
button	Built-in button control
separator	Separator control

Summary

Microsoft has made the most extensive and, arguably, the most constructive set of changes to Word 2007 over the previous versions. This chapter provided an overview of Microsoft Office Word 2007, and how it can be enhanced using VSTO 3.0. This chapter brings out the best part for all Office application developers using VSTO 3.0 and Visual Studio 2008.

Visual Studio 2008 has made the Word 2007 programming environment easier and faster for business enhancement. You can still assign custom functions to any command or macro through coding. You have learned the important objects of Word 2007. You have learned the concepts of document-level and application-level customization. You have learned, with examples, how to develop custom Actions Panes and Task Panes.

Finally, we explored the use of controls in a Word document, and learned how to add these controls at design time, bind them to data, and how to create them dynamically at run time. You have learned simple and complex data binding in Word 2007, with the help of sample code.

We then took a closer look at how to add host controls to a document host item, both at design time and at run time. You have learned about menus and Ribbon customization in Word 2007. We also looked at some of the special features of VSTO 3.0 such as host items, host controls, and the Ribbon.

4

Microsoft Office Excel Programming

Before we begin the chapter, let's see where you will stand once you complete reading this chapter on Microsoft Office Excel programming. Beginning with programming in Excel 2007 using VSTO 3.0 and proceeding with programming concepts, you will learn how to manipulate data inside Excel. Later, you will learn the concepts of workbook manipulation and worksheet manipulation, with code samples. When programming in the Excel 2007, the object model plays an important role. You will learn the most important and widely used objects, with the help of demonstrations.

In this chapter, you will learn:

- Excel 2007 in Visual Studio 2008, including how to start an Excel solution in Visual Studio 2008
- Excel 2007 solution: the object model, and the object model functional area
- Data and worksheet manipulation in Excel 2007
- Data processing with Microsoft SQL Server 2008
- Working with ranges, cell unions, named ranges, and so on
- Working with host items in Excel, and charts
- Customization using host controls in Excel
- Working with regular expressions, formulae, and smart tags
- Worksheet protection in Excel 2007

Word content control support in Excel is one of the key features that every Office developer has to learn; all of these details will be dealt in this chapter more precisely. Programmatically creating and managing Excel smart tags using VSTO and Excel formulas will enhance your Excel with VSTO programming knowledge. Finally, you will learn the regular expression and workbook protection concepts in Excel programming.

Microsoft Office Excel is the most frequently-used Microsoft application and one of the leading spreadsheet programs available. A spreadsheet program is a program that uses a huge grid to display data in rows and columns. The spreadsheet program can then be used to do calculation, data manipulation, and various similar tasks, against this data.

Programming in Excel

Microsoft Office Excel is one of the powerful Office tools that provides uncomplicated data management. It is loaded with features such as graphing, charting, pivot tables, and calculation. Even though Excel is loaded with numerous features for users, there may be some functionality that cannot be achieved by using the standard Microsoft Excel environment. In Microsoft Office Excel 2007, automation is a great mechanism for populating business documents (for example, reports) with data from backend system. This can be achieved by using VSTO 3.0 and Visual Studio 2008. Microsoft Office Excel 2007 is more programmable than ever before with support for Visual Studio Tools for Office.

VSTO is aimed at Microsoft Office Excel users who want to develop Excel-based applications for other Microsoft Office Excel users. VSTO 3.0 is shipped with all of the newly-enhanced Excel objects, including improved features for building Microsoft Office based solutions.

VSTO 3.0 is loaded with new features, including support for Windows form controls from within Microsoft Office tools customization. It provides the support for using .NET frameworks, objects and classes for Microsoft Office tools customization. For example, `System.Data` is the .NET frameworks object that can be used inside the Excel solution to process database operations. This new feature is tightly integrated with the Visual Studio 2008 IDE and gives you the comfort of design time customization of Excel documents for data display and UI customization.

Similar to other Microsoft Office Tools, with Microsoft Office Excel 2007 customization using VSTO 3.0, you have two levels of customization—document-level customization and application-level customization. Document-level customization is a solution created for document-level programming and is specific to the document that is part of that particular solution. Application-level customization is a solution created for application-level programming and is specific to the application, and therefore common to all documents based on that application.

In a simple **Hello World** demonstration, let's learn about the document level customization approach. We'll step through a simple task, showing how to create an Excel document that will display a **Hello World** message on startup.

Hello World example using Visual Studio 2008

1. Open Visual Studio 2008, and create a new **Excel 2007 Workbook** project.

2. Select **New Project**. Under **Office** select **2007**, and then select the **Excel 2007 Workbook** template and name the project **ExcelHelloWorld**, as shown in the following image:

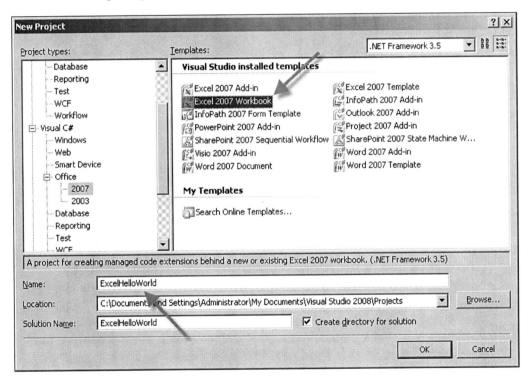

3. The document selection dialog box is displayed. At this point, you need to choose the template for your design. In this example, you select a new blank template and click on the **OK** button. Refer to the following screenshot:

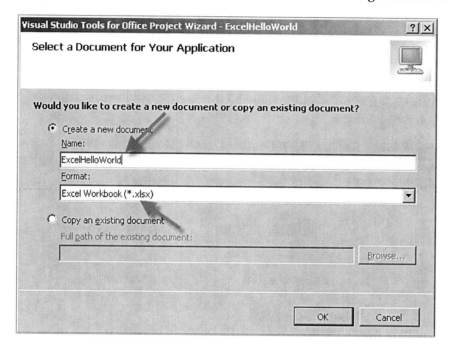

4. The solution will be created with all of the supporting files required for our development of an Excel solution. Each solution is created with three worksheets, with default names: Sheet1, Sheet2, and Sheet3 for the workbook you're going to customize , as shown in the following image. The number of sheets in a new workbook depends on the settings in Excel. The following image also shows you the Excel-supported controls, placed on the leftmost side of the Visual Studio 2008 toolbox panel. You can also see the visual representation of Excel 2007 inside Visual Studio 2008.

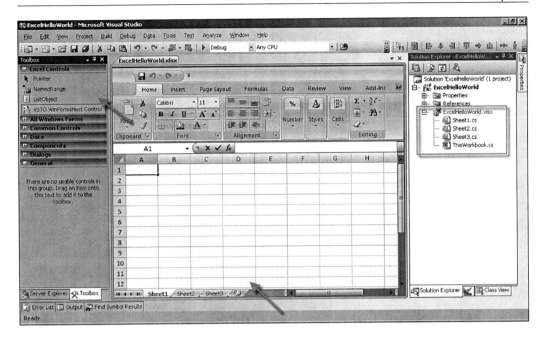

5. Let's write our **Hello World** message in a cell when we load the Excel 2007 document. Write the following code inside the `ThisWorkbook.cs` file.

```
// The Startup event of workbook in our Excel solution
// Startup event common to all Office application
// Startup event will be fired at the start of the application

private void ThisWorkbook_Startup(object sender,
    System.EventArgs e)
{
// Creating the instance of active WorkSheet of Excel Document

    Excel.Worksheet AuthorWorkSheet = ThisApplication.ActiveSheet
    as Excel.Worksheet;

// Get the range using number index through Excel cells
    by setting AuthorExchange to an Excel range object starting at
    (1,1) and ending at (1,1)
```

```
      Excel.Range AuthorExcelRange = ThisApplication.
         get_Range(AuthorWorkSheet.Cells[1, 1],
         AuthorWorkSheet.Cells[1, 1]);

   // Setting the value in the cell

      AuthorExcelRange.Value2 = "Hello! this is my VSTO program for
      Excel 2007";

   }
```

The following screenshot results after adding and executing the preceding code:

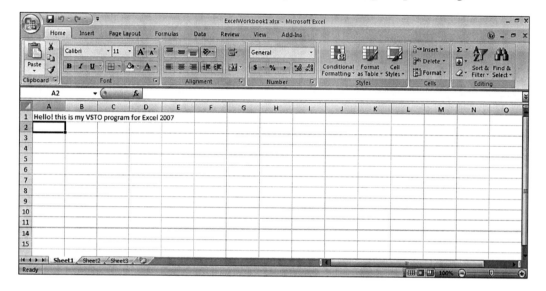

Manipulation

Microsoft Office Excel is one of the most comprehensive data management tools for all kinds of users. It is a tool that can be easily understood and quickly learnt. The most important feature of Microsoft Office Excel is its capability to manipulate data from different sources.

Excel is one of the most powerful and user-friendly data manipulation applications. You could use Excel to predict what's ahead for your business by creating detailed financial forecasts. This powerful application has pivot table functionality that allows you to drop in your data and rearrange it to answer all kinds of business data analysis type questions. Excel helps you to build various useful analytical tools such as your monthly sales report and product sales growth analysis more easily and flexibly. Excel offers you formulae and functions that will help you to perform complex financial calculations without any manual errors. Excel can provide you with a graphical presentation of your business data by using charts and graphs.

Want to know your growth levels for a specific product sales range? Check which parts of your business are performing worse? The pivot table provides more information from your business in depth.

Every application in this computer world works with data. The data can be in any form and can belong to different sources. The key question for data management is where to place the data. You manage the data in two ways: data managed outside the program and data managed inside the program. The data managed outside the program includes data managed in a database, a file system, and so on. Data managed inside the program includes data in different worksheets within the workbook, embedded images, and so on.

Data manipulation

For users who are not satisfied with the default features in Microsoft Office Excel, VSTO programming makes Excel more flexible, and provides a development tool for the creation of custom solutions for data manipulation and data analysis.

Custom programming using VSTO 3.0 improves most part of the Microsoft Office Excel solution. Custom programming using VSTO 3.0 provides a wide range of advantages, including saving time by automating most of the frequently-performed tasks, reducing errors due to manual operations, as well as enforcing standards for data processing, and building the capability to seamlessly integrate with other applications seamlessly.

Reading worksheet cells

There are many ways to manipulate data and write to the cells in an Excel worksheet. Let's see some of these ways.

We can read worksheet cells directly through the `Cells` property of the sheets, rows, and columns, and can set a value directly by using the cell's row and column index.

Open Visual Studio 2008 and create a new Excel solution. Refer to the previous example for full instructions of how to do this. Write the following code inside the `ThisWorkbook.cs` file. In this sample explanation, you are writing data into the worksheet by using the `Cells` object.

```
// The Startup event of workbook in our Excel solution
private void ThisWorkbook_Startup(object sender,
    System.EventArgs e)
{
// Set value for Cells row and column index
```

```
// Text data in Sheet1 cells
    Globals.Sheet1.Cells[3, 3] = "Set my data";
}
```

We can also read the worksheet and write data to the cells by using the `Range` object. In this case, you are creating the range and setting the text data for the range in the Excel worksheet.

Open Visual Studio 2008 and create a new solution, as before. Write the following code inside the `ThisWorkbook.cs` file. In this demonstration, you read the worksheet through the range of cells and set the value by reading through cell ranges.

```
private void ThisWorkbook_Startup(object sender,
    System.EventArgs e)
{
// Setting value in ExcelSheet cells through reading range object
    Excel.Range AuthorExcelSheetRange = Globals.Sheet1.Range["A2",
        "B2"];
// Text data for the range A2 to B2
    AuthorExcelSheetRange.Value2 = "Set my data";
}
```

Let's see a demonstration of how to read data from an external data file and display this inside our Excel cells. In this demonstration, you will see how the data from the text (`.txt`) file is displayed in the spreadsheet.

Opening a text file as a workbook using VSTO

We'll now see how to open the text file as a workbook by using VSTO and C# programming. This saves time and makes the user more comfortable in accessing the text file while processing the data. Open Visual Studio 2008 and create a new solution, as before. Write the following code inside the `ThisWorkbook.cs` file:

```
// Opening Text file as workbook
private void ThisWorkbook_Startup(object sender,
    System.EventArgs e)
{
// In the workbook objects, file path as parameter in Opentext
 property this.Application.Workbooks.OpenText(@"C:\TechBooks.txt",
// Value 1 is, the row from which it will read data in the text
    file missing, 1,
```

```
// Checks for delimits for text parsing
    Excel.XlTextParsingType.xlDelimited,
// Text Enumeration value
    Excel.XlTextQualifier.xlTextQualifierNone,
    missing, missing, missing, true, missing, missing, missing,
    missing, missing, missing, missing, missing, missing);
}
```

Connecting with Microsoft SQL Server 2008 database

Microsoft SQL Server 2008 is a relational database management system developed by Microsoft Corporation. Microsoft SQL Server is used to manage a huge volume of data along with relation and Metadata information for this data. VSTO provides support for manipulating the data from your database inside Excel using **ADO.NET** classes.

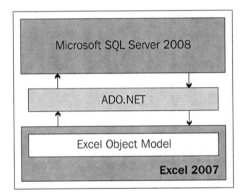

The preceding figure demonstrates how an Excel 2007 object is used to interact with the Microsoft SQL Server database. Let's see how to connect with a relational database management system, retrieve data from the database, and finally display it in our Excel spreadsheet. This demonstration shows you how to retrieve data from a Microsoft SQL Server 2008 database and place the retrieved data into the worksheet cells.

Open Visual Studio 2008 and create a new solution, as usual. Write the following code inside the ThisWorkbook.cs file.

```
// Namespace for SQL Server connection
    using System.Data.SqlClient;
// Startup event of the workbook
    private void ThisWorkbook_Startup(object sender,
        System.EventArgs e)
```

```
{
    // Opening SQL connection for Microsoft SQL Server 2008
    // WINNER the database server contains the databse called Products
        SqlConnection MySQLConnection = new SqlConnection(@"Data
            Source=WINNER;Initial Catalog=Products;
            Integrated Security=True");

    // Passing SQL command text
        SqlCommand MySQLCommand = new SqlCommand("SELECT * FROM
        Books", MySQLConnection);
        MySQLConnection.Open();

    // SQL reader to read through data from Database
        SqlDataReader MySQLReader = MySQLCommand.ExecuteReader();

    // Get the active sheet of current application
        Excel.Worksheet MyWorkSheet = this.Application.ActiveSheet as
            Excel.Worksheet;

    // Header for the columns set in the Value2 properties
        ((Excel.Range)MyWorkSheet.Cells[1, 1]).Value2 = "Book Name";
        ((Excel.Range)MyWorkSheet.Cells[1, 2]).Value2 = "Author Name";

    // Indexer
        int i = 2;

    // Loop to read through the database returned data
        while (MySQLReader.Read())
        {
        // Writing the data from the database table column BookName
            ((Excel.Range)MyWorkSheet.Cells[i, 1]).Value2 =
                MySQLReader["BookName"];

        // Writing the data from the database table column Author
            ((Excel.Range)MyWorkSheet.Cells[i, 2]).Value2 =
                MySQLReader["Author"];
            i++;
        }
    // Dispose the SQL command
        MySQLCommand.Dispose();

    // Closing SQL connection after using it.
        MySQLConnection.Close();
}
```

The following screenshot displays data retrieved from Microsoft SQL Server 2008 database and the data being displayed in the worksheet cells.

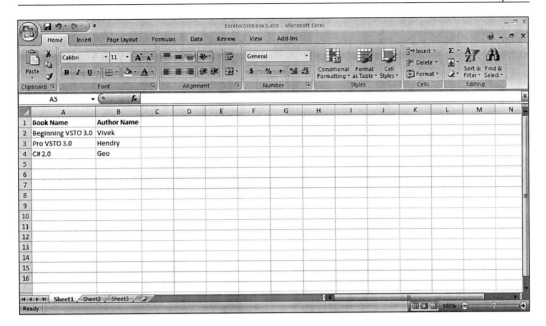

In this demonstration, you learned how to connect with a Microsoft SQL Server 2008 database in order to get data and populate it in a workbook. This is just one of the ways of manipulating data outside of a workbook.

Worksheet manipulation

A Microsoft Excel file is represented in Excel as a workbook. Each and every workbook can have many worksheets. Worksheets are individual data grids within the workbook. The term 'worksheet' refers to the rows and columns of the sheet on which you are working, whereas the term 'spreadsheet' refers to a type of computer application.

VSTO helps you to manage Excel worksheets programmatically. Using VSTO's programming support, you can access worksheets, add worksheets, delete worksheets, and so on.

Open Visual Studio 2008 and create a solution with all the supporting files for the development of the Excel solution. Write the following code inside the `ThisWorkbook.cs` file. Here, you're going to add and delete worksheets within your workbook, at runtime, using the VSTO programming.

- Code for adding a worksheet to your workbook using VSTO:

```
private void ThisWorkbook_Startup(object sender,
    System.EventArgs e)
{
```

```
// Adding worksheet to our workbook
    Excel.Worksheet AuthorWorksheet = Sheets.Add (missing,
        missing, 1, missing) as Excel.Worksheet;
}
```

- Code for deleting a worksheet from a workbook using VSTO:

```
private void ThisWorkbook_Startup(object sender,
    System.EventArgs e)
{
// Code to delete the second sheet, referenced here as Sheets[2]
    because we have not turned off the DisplayAlerts flag, a
    warning message will be prompted before deleting
    which causes a stop in the automated solution that requires
    user input
    ((Excel.Worksheet)this.Application.ActiveWorkbook.
        Sheets[2]).Delete();

}
```

The following screenshot shows how the code tries to delete the worksheet and how the Excel application prompts the user to confirm the deletion.

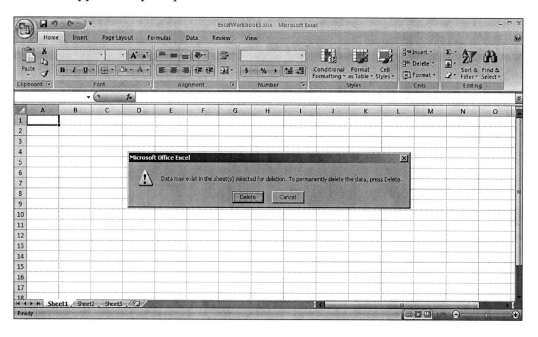

The following programming tip will help you to avoid seeing the delete warning message that is displayed to the user when deleting the worksheet.

```
// To avoid warning messages
    this.Application.DisplayAlerts = false;
```

```
// The code will delete the second sheet.
    ((Excel.Worksheet)this.Application.ActiveWorkbook.Sheets[2]).
        Delete();
```

Worksheet manipulation helps document users to provide better data processing. It is advantageous as it has easy access to data, builds better user interfaces, and optimizes data processing for reports and other business needs.

Working with ranges

Microsoft Office Excel is loaded with a wide variety of objects that can be programmed for using VSTO 3.0. The Range object is probably the most frequently-used object in the Excel object model, and helps an Excel developer to manipulate the cells and their data by using a referenced range. In this section, we will see how to refer to cells programmatically, and manipulate the ranges of data in Microsoft Office Excel 2007. The Excel range is a vital part of the Excel application. A range may correspond to a logical relationship between cells.

The following sample program explains how to read the cells of a worksheet by using the Range object, and how to format the background color of a range of cells.

Open Visual Studio 2008 and create a new solution, as before. Write the following code inside the Sheet1.cs file.

```
private void Sheet1_Startup(object sender, System.EventArgs e)
{

// Reading Excel using Range object
    Excel.Range AuthorRange = Globals.Sheet1.Range["A1", "C5"] as
        Excel.Range;

// Formatting the selected Range with autocolor format
    AuthorRange.AutoFormat(Excel.XlRangeAutoFormat.
        xlRangeAutoFormatColor1, true, false, true, false,
        true, true);

}
```

Adding and executing the preceding code results in the following screenshot:

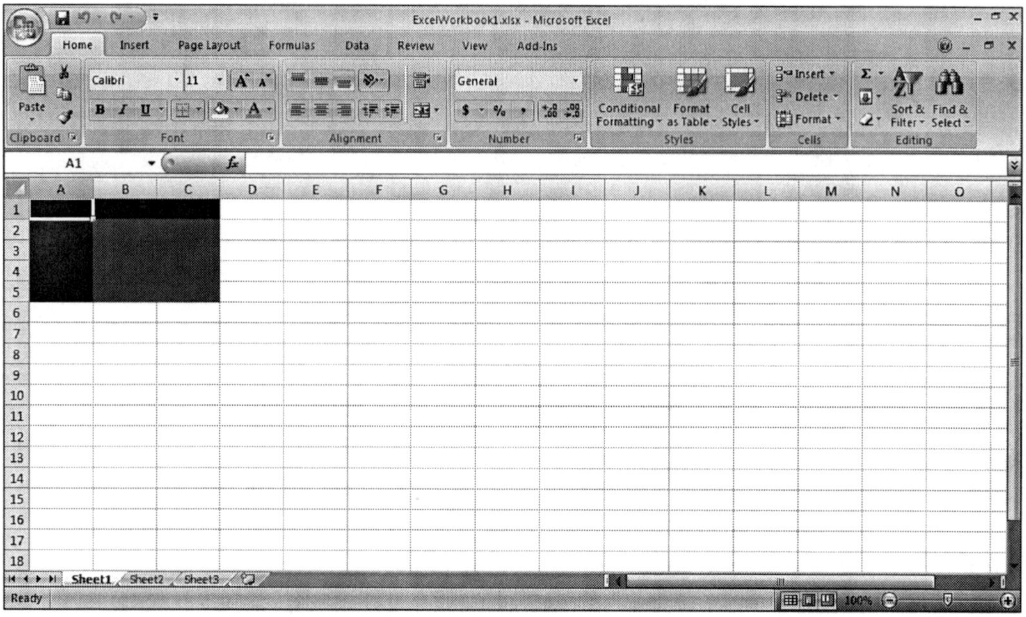

Cells

In any spreadsheet program, such as Microsoft Office Excel, each rectangular box is referred to as a cell. A cell is the intersection point of a column and a row inside the spreadsheet. Using VSTO, you can manipulate the cells in the worksheet for processing data in the worksheet. You can apply formulas, add smart tags, and merge and format cells, depending on conditions.

In the following example, you will see how to merge a cell in the worksheet by using the Range object, and also how to use the copy operation by using the Range object in the Excel object model.

Open Visual Studio 2008 and create a new solution, as before. Write the following code inside the Sheet1.cs file:

```
private void Sheet1_Startup(object sender, System.EventArgs e)
{
// Merging the cell of provided range using cell ranges
    Globals.Sheet1.get_Range("A1:A5,B1:B5",
    missing).Merge(missing);
// Copy the range of cells and put in another range of cell
    Globals.Sheet1.Range["C5", missing].Copy(Range["D5",
    missing]);
}
```

As we can see in the following screenshot, we merged two cells and copied the contents of the cell **C5** to cell **D5**.

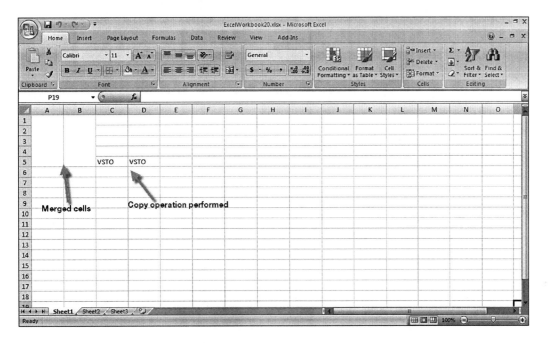

Unions

A combination of ranges has to be treated as single range, and that range is referred to as the **Union**. In other words, the display of a group of ranges in a combined format is called a Union. Unions make it easy for the developer to process data inside a worksheet. Generally, a Union is used to calculate a subtotal.

Open Visual Studio 2008 and create a new solution, as usual. Write the following code inside the Sheet1.cs file:

```
private void Sheet1_Startup(object sender, System.EventArgs e)
{
// Creating Range object instance
    Excel.Range AuthorRange1 = this.Application.get_Range("B5",
        missing);

// Creating another Range object instance
    Excel.Range AuthorRange2 = this.Application.get_Range("C5",
        missing);

// Using Union method of current Excel
    Excel.Range AuthorRange3 = this.Application.
        Union(AuthorRange1, AuthorRange2, missing, missing,
```

```
                missing, missing, missing, missing, missing, missing,
                missing, missing, missing, missing, missing, missing,
                missing, missing, missing, missing, missing, missing,
                missing, missing, missing, missing, missing, missing,
                missing, missing);
// Writing the new range using the union operation
    AuthorRange3.Value2 = "Programming VSTO Book";
}
```

Named ranges

Named ranges are used as replacements for the columns of numbers in Excel spreadsheet. You can use a more indicative name to refer to a column of numbers. Such ranges are known as Named ranges.

Open Visual Studio 2008 and create a new solution, as usual. Write the following code inside the `Sheet1.cs` file:

```
// Instance of the NamedRange Class
Microsoft.Office.Tools.Excel.NamedRange AuthorNamedRange = null;
private void Sheet1_Startup(object sender, System.EventArgs e)
{
// Setting range of cells from E1 to G1
    Excel.Range AuthorRange = this.Range["E1", "G1"];

// Setting the range name for cells
    AuthorNamedRange = this.Controls.AddNamedRange(AuthorRange,
        "AuthorCells");

// Updating the values in the cell
    AuthorNamedRange.Value2 = "VSTO - My First Book";
}
```

The following screenshot shows the results of adding and executing the preceding code:

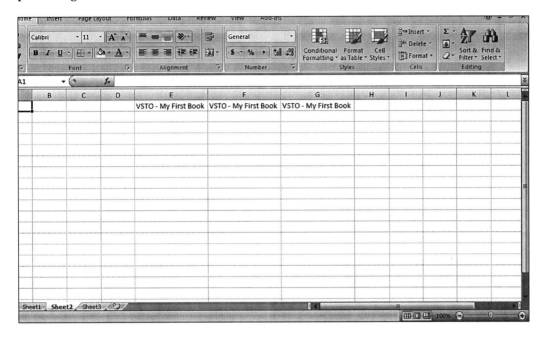

Excel host items

Excel host items are classes that offer programming models for developing document-level solutions using VSTO. Document-level customization uses a set of host items that includes `Microsoft.Office.Tools.Excel.Worksheet`. Worksheet host is one of the host items that acts as a container for controls such as Windows form controls.

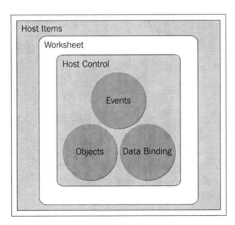

In Excel, you have three types of host items:

- Workbook
- Worksheet
- ChartSheet

In every Excel solution, there is one workbook host item and a separate worksheet host item for each worksheet in the workbook. All of these host items are folded in the native Excel workbook, Excel worksheet, and the Excel ChartSheet, which together constitute the `Microsoft.Office.Interop.Excel` namespace.

The workbook host item

A workbook host item is created whenever you create an Excel 2007 workbook project using Visual Studio 2008, that is, document-level customization for Microsoft Office Excel. Visual Studio Tools for Office, by design, creates a workbook host item within the project solution. When programming, you need to reference the workbook using the `ThisWorkbook` object. The workbook host item is a workbook object model, which is available in the VSTO Excel object model.

There are numerous events exposed in the workbook host item. You will see some of these events in the sample code below. In this example, you're going to see the sample work for the `NewWorkbook` event in an Excel workbook. First let's see the `NewWorkbook` event for the workbook host item. Here, let's register the `NewWorkbook` event in the workbook solution. Within Office 2007 tools such as Excel 2007 and other Office applications, there is an option to handle events by using the **Event Manager**. The Event Manager provides mechanisms by which forms or documents can provide and respond to events. The Event Manager is called from the `InternalStartup()` method which in turn controls the events that are registered when a document is initially loaded. Each captured event can be registered within the `InternalStartup()` method, and then the delegates can be constructed to encapsulate a reference to a method that handles the events' custom code.

Open Visual Studio 2008 and create a new solution, as usual. Write the following code inside the `ThisWorkbook.cs` file:

```
private void InternalStartup()
{
// Explicitly cast the application object to the application
   events
    ((Excel.AppEvents_Event)ThisApplication).NewWorkbook += new
        Microsoft.Office.Interop.Excel.
      AppEvents_NewWorkbookEventHandler(ThisWorkbook_
        NewWorkbook);
```

```
// Visual Studio generated
    this.Startup += new System.EventHandler(ThisWorkbook_Startup);
    this.Shutdown += new System.EventHandler(ThisWorkbook_
        Shutdown);
}

// NewWorkbook event in the Excel solution
public void ThisWorkbook_NewWorkbook(Microsoft.Office.
    Interop.Excel.Workbook AuthorWorkBook)
{
// Reading from Excel using the Range object
    Excel.Range AuthorRange = Globals.Sheet1.Range["B1", "D5"] as
        Excel.Range;
// Formatting the selected Range with autocolor format
    AuthorRange.AutoFormat(Excel.XlRangeAutoFormat.
        xlRangeAutoFormatClassic3, true, false, true, false, true,
        true);
// Messagebox after range of cells formatted
    MessageBox.Show("New workbook name:  " + AuthorWorkBook.Name);
}
```

Now, let's see the WorkbookOpen event of the workbook host item. Here, let's register the WorkbookOpen event in the workbook solution.

```
private void InternalStartup()
{
// Explicitly cast the application object to the application
    events
    ((Excel.AppEvents_Event)ThisApplication).WorkbookOpen += new
    Microsoft.Office.Interop.Excel.
    AppEvents_WorkbookOpenEventHandler(ThisWorkbook_WorkbookOpen);

// Visual Studio generated
    this.Startup += new System.EventHandler(ThisWorkbook_Startup);
    this.Shutdown += new System.EventHandler(ThisWorkbook_
        Shutdown);
}

// Open event of Workbook
    public void ThisWorkbook_WorkbookOpen(Microsoft.Office.
        Interop.Excel.Workbook AuthorWorkBook)
{
// Messagebox shows the name of the file being opened
    MessageBox.Show("You are opening workbook name:  " +
        AuthorWorkBook.Name);
}
```

The worksheet host item

A worksheet host item is the worksheet in the Excel workbook. You can have more than one worksheet in your workbook. This is an object that exposes events and works as a holder for components. You can add Windows forms controls to the host item, just as you would add them to your Windows forms. Worksheets are the key components of any kind of Excel solution.

The following example will show how to program for the Change event of the cells in the Excel worksheet. Open Visual Studio 2008 and create a new solution, as before. Write the following code inside the `ThisWorkbook.cs` file. This will register the Change event in the worksheet host item's `.cs` file:

```
// Visual studio generated InternalStartup()
private void InternalStartup()
{
// Register your Change event
    this.Change += new Microsoft.Office.Interop.Excel.
        DocEvents_ChangeEventHandler(Sheet1_Change);
}
```

The following code should be placed inside the Change event of the worksheet host item:

```
private void Sheet1_Change(Excel.Range AuthorCellPoint)
{
// Reading the current context of cell which has been changed
    string AuthorCellChanged = AuthorCellPoint.
        get_Address(missing, missing,Excel.XlReferenceStyle.xlA1,
        missing, missing);

// Message displaying the changed cell address
    MessageBox.Show("The Cell " + this.Name + " : " +
        AuthorCellChanged + " is changed.");

}
```

Once the code is executed, you'll get a confirmation message in a message box, as shown in the following screenshot:

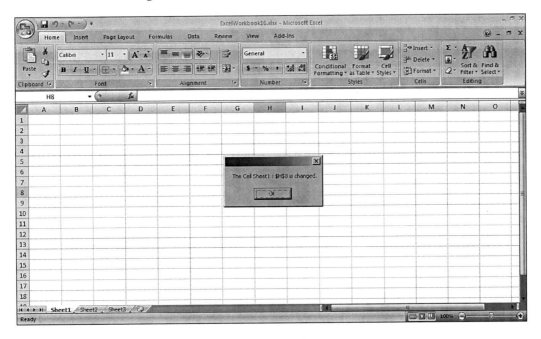

The ChartSheet host item

A ChartSheet host item is a worksheet in an Excel workbook that presents information in the form of charts and graphs. The ChartSheet host item contains only charts, and exposes some events. You cannot add any controls inside the ChartSheet host item even though it is a worksheet in an Excel workbook. The ChartSheet host item works as a holder for components.

In a document-level customization project, you cannot create host items at run time. Another limitation is that when you create a new worksheet host item at run time using the add method, you get a native `Microsoft.Office.Interop.Excel` worksheet object rather than a `Microsoft.Office.Tools.Excel` worksheet host item. There are numerous events exposed in the ChartSheet host item. You will see some of these events in the following sample code.

Let's see a demonstration of the `MouseUp` event of the ChartSheet host item.

Open Visual Studio 2008 and create a new solution, as usual. Right-click on the **ExcelWorkbook.xlsx** file of your Excel 2007 solution in the **Solution Explorer**, and select **Add New Excel Chart**.

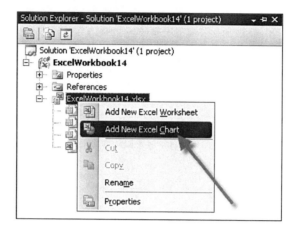

In the `Chart.cs` file, you can program your functionality. In this example, let's write a code for the `MouseUp` event in the ChartSheet host item:

```
// MouseUp event registration in the Chart Host item.
private void InternalStartup()
{
    this.MouseUp += new Microsoft.Office.Interop.Excel.
        ChartEvents_MouseUpEventHandler(Chart4_MouseUp);
}
private void Chart4_MouseUp(int Button, int Shift, int x, int y)
{
// Set the constant value for range of cells
    Globals.Sheet1.Range["B2", "B4"].Value2 = 15;
    Globals.Sheet1.Range["C2", "C4"].Value2 = 18;
// Adding the sheet1 cells as data source
    this.SetSourceData(Globals.Sheet1.Range["B2", "C4"],
        Excel.XlRowCol.xlColumns);
// Chart display type
    this.ChartType = Excel.XlChartType.xlConeColStacked100;
// Message to display the mouse moved
    MessageBox.Show("Your clicked at X-axis: " + x.ToString() + "
        and Y-axis: " + y.ToString());
}
```

The following screenshot shows the results of adding and executing the preceding code:

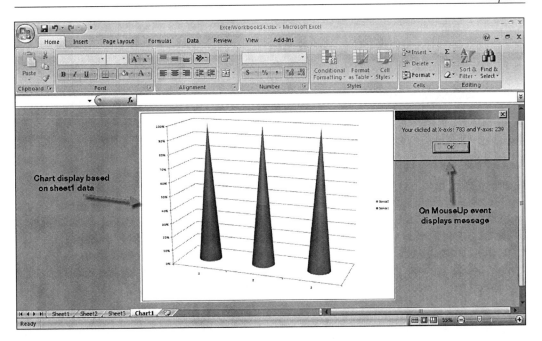

The Excel host items are loaded with many features that help Office developers to build optimized Excel solutions. Even though the Excel host item has many features, it has a few drawbacks when using Excel host items for programming.

Excel host controls

The member variables of the base classes that are created when you add bookmarks, named ranges, list objects, and so on to Excel are called as host controls in the Excel object model. VSTO has improved a number of objects in the Excel 2007 object model, such as the capability to bind data to an object. You can also expose the object's events. These objects are called Excel host items and Excel host controls. Microsoft .NET-friendly classes, which are built on top of the native Office objects, are meant to be host controls. Some Office developers refer to these controls as the content controls of Excel. These controls provide you with a wide variety of data formatting, and give fine development control to developers, in order to provide better presentation of data for Excel users.

In general, host controls have some basic functionality, as Office objects are based on some enhanced features, such as richer event models and data binding capabilities. The host controls can be added to and deleted from your Excel documents programmatically. Host controls are of the type `Microsoft.Office.Tools.Excel` and the corresponding native objects are of the type `Microsoft.Office.Interop.Excel`.

The following Excel host controls are available in the Excel object model:

- `Chart` control
- `ListObject` control
- `NamedRange` control
- `XMLMappedRange` control

Chart control

The `Chart` control is the `Chart` object of the object model. The `Chart` control can process simple data binding. The `Chart` control exposes events to do more interactive operations over the control. An Excel `Chart` object is loaded with a large set of options, which will give the Office developers more flexibility in displaying data dynamically. Some of the key requirements that can be achieved though VSTO Excel objects are addressed here for your reference. It is possible for the Excel `Chart` object to create, destroy, and recreate operations dynamically.

The Excel `Chart` control has more events, in order to simplify interaction with users. Event procedures in Microsoft Office Excel 2007 have diverse levels of control and influence. Excel developers have to note that event procedures in an Excel worksheet's code unit detect only events in the Excel worksheet, whereas event procedures in a workbook's code unit can catch events that occur in all of the sheets within the workbook.

Let's see a small example that shows how to read the range of cell values and dynamically generate a chart inside the Excel worksheet.

Open Visual Studio 2008 and create a new solution, as before. Write the following code in the `Sheet1.cs` file:

```
private void Sheet1_Startup(object sender, System.EventArgs e)
{
// Chart control object
    Microsoft.Office.Tools.Excel.Chart AuthorBookInfo;
// Chart control properties to display
// parameters are chart display properties
    AuthorBookInfo = this.Controls.AddChart(75,90,550,150,
        "BookReport");
// Type of chart displayed based on the data
    AuthorBookInfo.ChartType = Excel.XlChartType.
        xlCylinderBarStacked;
// Set the constant value for range of cells
    Globals.Sheet1.Range["B1", "B5"].Value2 = 82;
    Globals.Sheet1.Range["D1", "D5"].Value2 = 83;
```

```
// Gets the cells that define the data to be charted.
    Excel.Range AuthorChartRange = this.get_Range("B1", "D5");
// Adding data source to the chart control
    AuthorBookInfo.SetSourceData(AuthorChartRange, missing);

}
```

The following screenshot shows the results of adding and executing the preceding code:

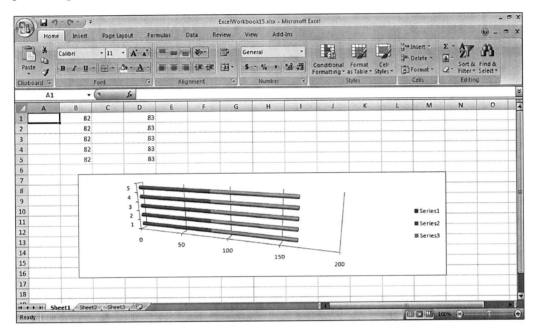

The ListObject control

ListObject is a control that holds the data as a list that exposes events. The ListObject control has the capability to perform complex data binding with different data sources. The ListObject control helps you to build a formatted visual data representation for the user. Let's take a look at an example:

Open Visual Studio 2008 and create a new solution, as usual. Write the following code in the Sheet1.cs file:

```
private void Sheet2_Startup(object sender, System.EventArgs e)
{
// ListObject is initialized
    Microsoft.Office.Tools.Excel.ListObject AuthorBookListObject;
// Adding the ListObject control to the sheet
    AuthorBookListObject = this.Controls.AddListObject(this.
```

```
          get_Range("$B$3:$F$9", missing), "AuthorBooksReport");
// Setting new style for ListObject
    AuthorBookListObject.TableStyle =
        Excel.XlTableStyleElementType.xlWholeTable;
}
```

As we can see in the following screenshot, we have added the ListObject control and we have set a new style for it.

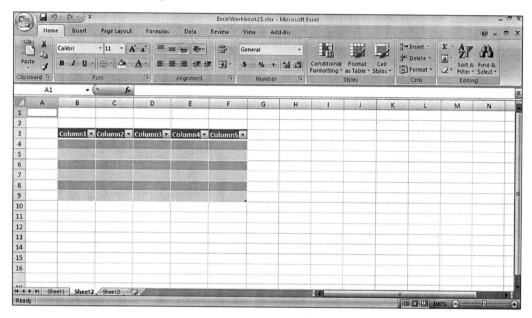

The NamedRange control

VSTO provides a new NamedRange control , which is used for representing named ranges in an Excel worksheet. Alternatively, you could say that the NamedRange control is the control in which a range of cells will have a unique name for identification purposes. When drawn onto a range of cells in the worksheet, the control creates a NamedRange object at the selected location. The NamedRange control exposes events, and has the capability to bind with data. The range is nothing but a collection of cells in the spreadsheet, that can be used to provide formatting and data binding.

Open Visual Studio 2008 and create a new solution, as usual. Write the following code in the Sheet1.cs file:

```
private void InternalStartup()
{
// BeforeDoubleClick event of the sheet
    this.BeforeDoubleClick += new Microsoft.Office.Interop.Excel.
```

```
            DocEvents_BeforeDoubleClickEventHandler(
            Sheet1_BeforeDoubleClick);
}

private void Sheet1_BeforeDoubleClick(Microsoft.Office.
    Interop.Excel.Range AuthorRange, ref bool Proceed)
{
// Setting the value in the cell
    Globals.Sheet1.Range["B2", missing].Value2 = "Buy VSTO Book";

// Formatting the color for the cell value
    Globals.Sheet1.Range["B2", missing].Font.Color =
        System.Drawing.ColorTranslator.ToOle(System.Drawing.Color.
        DarkGreen);

// Formatting the font style for the cell value
    Globals.Sheet1.Range["B2", missing].Font.Bold = true;
}
```

The XMLMappedRange control

The XMLMappedRange control supports simple data binding such as binding to a single data field. The Microsoft.Office.Tools.Excel.XMLMappedRange control can use the same formatting that you apply to a Microsoft.Office.Interop.Excel.Range.

The SelectionChange event

The SelectionChange event is raised when the cell related to the attribute is selected or deselected. To perform SelectionChange event registration in the Excel worksheet host item, open Visual Studio 2008 and create a new solution, as before. Write the following code in the Sheet1.cs file:

```
private void InternalStartup()
{

    this.SelectionChange += new Microsoft.Office.Interop.Excel.
        DocEvents_SelectionChangeEventHandler(
        Sheet1_SelectionChange);

}

private void Sheet1_SelectionChange(Excel.Range AuthorCellPoint)
{
// Reading the address of the cell selected
    string AuthorCellSelection = AuthorCellPoint.
        get_Address(missing,missing, Excel.XlReferenceStyle.xlA1,
        missing, missing);
```

```
    // The selected cell address is updated in a cell
        Globals.Sheet1.Range["B2", missing].Value2 =
            AuthorCellSelection;

}
```

The following screenshot shows the results of adding and executing the preceding code:

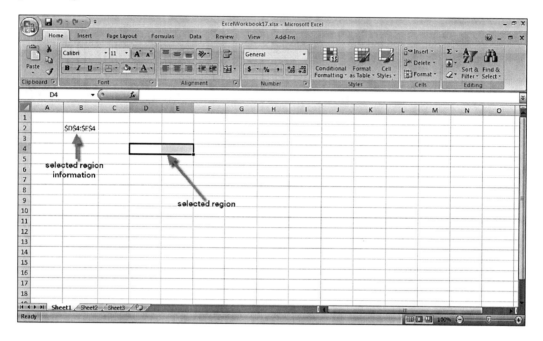

Creating Excel smart tags with VSTO

Smart tags are intended to identify particular data and then provide the action options available based on the data type identified. The actions are available via a button that becomes visible close to the cell that contains the data. The button is displayed when the cell is activated, or whenever you move the mouse pointer over the cell.

Smart tags are one of the most useful features that have been enhanced in VSTO 3.0. VSTO smart tags are much easier to use and easy to understand. You can easily customize the actions more strongly than with standard texts. Another good feature is that you have access to the Range object of the standard texts.

By default, smart tag functionality is turned off in Microsoft Office Excel 2007. VSTO smart tags can be used only in document-level projects for Excel 2007.

First, you need to turn on the smart tag recognition functionality. To do this, execute the following procedure.

Open Visual Studio 2008 and create a new solution, as usual. The following is the example code for adding smart tags using VSTO in the Excel solution. Add this code to the `Sheet1.cs` file:

```
private void Sheet1_Startup(object sender, System.EventArgs e)
{
// Adding the NamedRange for cells
    Microsoft.Office.Tools.Excel.NamedRange AuthorRange1 =
        this.Controls.AddNamedRange(this.Range["B2", missing],
        "AuthorRange1");

// Enabling SmartTag option in the workbook
    Globals.ThisWorkbook.SmartTagOptions.EmbedSmartTags = true;

// Enabling SmartTag recognizer
    Globals.ThisWorkbook.Application.SmartTagRecognizers.
        Recognize = true;

// Applying formula, MSFT is the Stock Quote for Microsoft
        Corporation
// The SmartTag for recognizing stock symbols
    AuthorRange1.Formula = "MSFT";

// SmartTags added to the action
    Excel.SmartTag AuthorSmartTag1 = AuthorRange1.SmartTags.
        Add("urn:schemas-microsoft-com:
            smarttags#StockTickerSymbol");

    Excel.SmartTag AuthorSmartTag2 = AuthorRange1.SmartTags.
        Add("urn:schemas-microsoft-com:smarttags#list");

}
```

The following screenshot shows the results of adding and executing the preceding code:

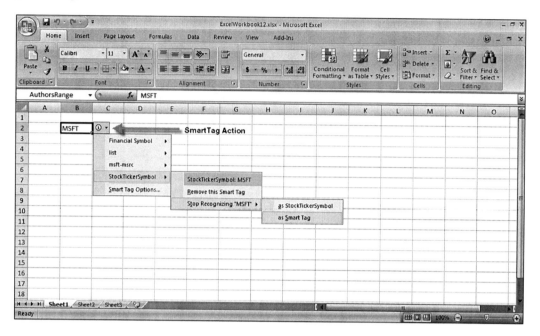

Excel has numerous built-in options for recognizers, which can be disabled and enabled as per the users' needs. In addition to this, VSTO offers an option to create and manage document-level smart tags. When creating smart tags using VSTO, first create the instance of the SmartTag class and provide the caption name and unique identifier for your smart tag. Using the methods and properties, you can precede the smart tag creation.

Excel formulae

Microsoft Office Excel formulae allow you to execute calculations on the data entered in the spreadsheet cells. Using a formula is a method of performing calculations that rely on a recognized approach. VSTO helps Office developers to automate Excel solutions with formulae for calculation in the cells of the spreadsheet.

Formula is a property of the NamedRange control in the Microsoft.Office.Tools. Excel object. If the NamedRange control contains a formula, the Formula property returns the formula as a string.

Let's see an example of multiplying a range of cell values, and displaying the results in the assigned cell. Open Visual Studio 2008 and create a new solution, as usual. Write the following code in the Sheet1.cs file:

```
private void Sheet2_Startup(object sender, System.EventArgs e)
{
// Range of cell for calculation
    Microsoft.Office.Tools.Excel.NamedRange AuthorCellRange1 =
        this.Controls.AddNamedRange(this.Range["B1", "B2"],
        "AuthorNamedRange1");
// Cell range to display the calculated result
    Microsoft.Office.Tools.Excel.NamedRange AuthorCellRange2 =
        this.Controls.AddNamedRange(this.Range["B3", missing],
        "AuthorNamedRange2");
// Default value for the cells
    AuthorCellRange1.Value2 = 10;
// Formula to multiply the cell values
    AuthorCellRange2.Formula = "=B1*B2";
// Formula hiding property for protected sheets
    AuthorCellRange2.FormulaHidden = true;
// Calculate the cell values
    AuthorCellRange2.Calculate();
}
```

The following screenshot shows the results of adding and executing the
preceding code:

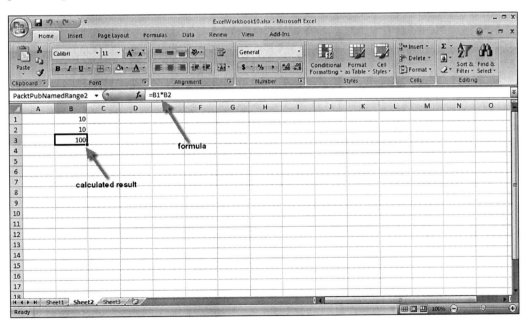

The preceding example shows the implementation of the simple multiplication formula for two cells in the worksheet. You can perform more complex and challenging calculations using this formula in Excel. Applying the formulae using VSTO brings you the great advantage of applying them at runtime, and also based on conditions.

Regular expressions

Regular expressions give a short, flexible, and snappy way of recognizing strings of text, such as characters, words, or patterns. There is no specific feature available in VSTO 3.0 for regular expressions. VSTO allows you to use most of the .NET framework's namespaces and classes. In VSTO, you can use regular expression with the help of .NET programming.

The following is an example for email validation applied to an Excel cell using regular expression techniques for the Excel 2007 document-level solution.

Open Visual Studio 2008 and create a new solution with all the supporting files for the development of the Excel solution. Write the following code in the Sheet1.cs file:

```csharp
private void Sheet1_Startup(object sender, System.EventArgs e)
{
// Setting the value in the cell
    Globals.Sheet1.Range["A1", missing].Value2 =
        "vivek@arimaan.com";
// Loading the cell value to the string
    string strCellData = Globals.Sheet1.Range["A1",
        missing].Value2.ToString();
// Validating the RegEx for email string
    if (EmailValidate(strCellData) == true)
    {
        // String display in the cell
        Globals.Sheet1.Range["B1", missing].Value2 =
            "Email Address is Valid";
    }
    else
    {
        // String display in the cell
        Globals.Sheet1.Range["B1", missing].Value2 =
            "Email Address is Not Valid";
    }
}
// Regular Expression validation function
```

```
public static bool EmailValidate(string strEmail)
{
    string strRegex = @"^([a-zA-Z0-9_\-\.]+)@((\[[0-9]{1,3}" +
        @"\.[0-9]{1,3}\.[0-9]{1,3}\.)|(([a-zA-Z0-9\-]+\" + @".)+))(" +
        [a-zA-Z]{2,4}|[0-9]{1,3})(\]?)$";
    Regex emailRegEx = new Regex(strRegex);
    if (emailRegEx.IsMatch(strEmail))
    {
        return (true);
    }
    else
    {
        return (false);
    }
}
```

The following screenshot shows the results of adding and executing the preceding code:

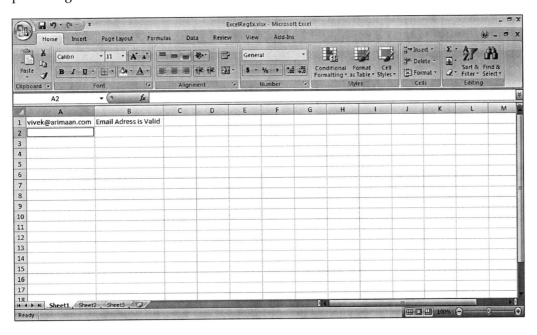

Regular expressions are used to find frequent occurrences of a pattern of characters within a string. These characters are of two types—one that includes alphabetic characters and numerals, called literal characters, and one that includes special characters such as * or @ or #. In the previous example, a regular expression was implemented using smart tags. You can also implement regular expressions via other controls and events, and not just through smart tags.

Excel data protection

Microsoft Office Excel provides a few layers of security and protection that allow you to control the access to an Excel document. VSTO offers a much wider variety of data and content protection options. One of the important concepts is authentication via a password request in order to access the data in the workbook. However, there are no out-of-the-box options available in VSTO to validate the strength of the password assigned to the workbook or worksheet.

Workbook protection

The best way of protecting an Excel document is to protect your entire Excel file with an access password, which will allow only authorized users to view or modify the data inside the workbook.

`Password` is a property of the Excel workbook class. You can access this property via the `Globals.ThisWorkbook.Password` property. You have more options available for password encryption when developing a protected Excel solution. Let's take a look at an example.

Open Visual Studio 2008 and create a new solution, as before. Write the following code inside the `ThisWorkbook.cs` file:

```
private void ThisWorkbook_Startup(object sender,
    System.EventArgs e)
{
// Prompting the Textbox to enter the new password for your
    workbook
    string AuthorPassword = this.Application.
        InputBox("New Password:", missing, missing, missing,
        missing, missing, missing, missing).ToString();
// Check the Password is not empty
    if (AuthorPassword == string.Empty)
    {
// If password is empty show message
        MessageBox.Show("Please enter valid password");
    }
    else
    {
// Else set the password to the Workbooks password property
        Globals.ThisWorkbook.Password = AuthorPassword;
    }
}
```

The following screenshot shows the results of adding and executing the preceding code:

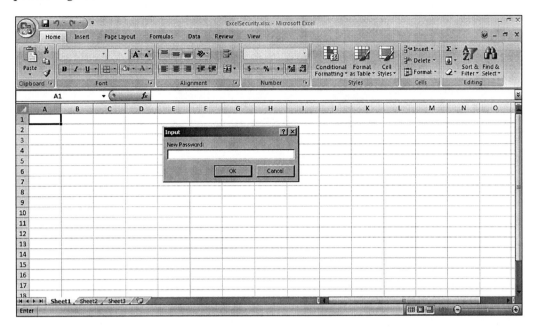

When you try to click on the **OK** button without entering any password information, an error message will be displayed, as shown in the following screenshot:

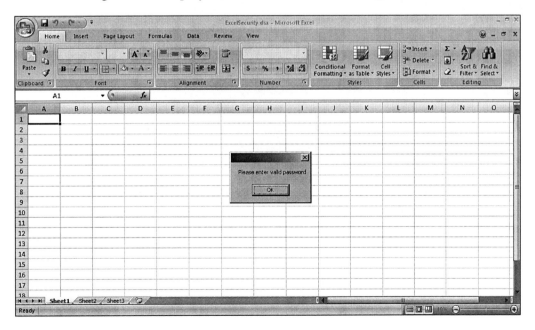

Worksheet protection

Worksheet protection is useful in many scenarios. A workbook may contain more than one worksheet and if the owner of the workbook wants to protect or hide one or more specific worksheets from other users then it can be done in Microsoft Office Excel.

Let's see how to protect the worksheet from public users with the help of a password.

Open Visual Studio 2008 and create a new solution, as before. Write the following code inside the `ThisWorkbook.cs` file:

```
private void Sheet1_Startup(object sender, System.EventArgs e)
{
    // This will protect the Worksheet with password from
        editing by the public users
    Globals.Sheet1.Protect("MyPassword", missing, missing,
        missing, missing, missing, missing, missing, missing,
        missing, missing, missing, missing, true, missing,
        missing);
}
```

In this section, you have learned the basic concepts of protecting the workbook and worksheet using VSTO and C# programming. You can also implement a custom algorithm for password security to tighten the strength of protection.

Summary

In this chapter, we focused on the basic functionality of the Microsoft Office Excel 2007 spreadsheet application. At the beginning of this chapter, we discussed data manipulation, Excel workbooks, and Excel worksheet manipulation. We have seen several ways of data processing through VSTO and C# in Microsoft Office Excel 2007, to help you learn the flexible ways of data processing for Excel. Reading further, you learned the concept of the object model in Excel and more about the Range object in the Excel object model. This chapter covered significant features for working with cells using Range objects. In the later part of the chapter, we learned more about how smart tags can be created using VSTO. This chapter also covered Excel host items and Excel host controls. We took a look at events that are exposed by Excel host items, with code snippets. We learned how VSTO helps Office developers to build Excel solutions with all of the basic features such as formulae and expressions. And, finally we saw how to secure an Excel workbook using VSTO.

5
Microsoft Office Outlook Programming

Microsoft Office Outlook is one of the world's most widely-used personal information management tool. Primarily, the Microsoft Office Outlook serves as an email application for a wide range of users. In this chapter, you will learn the concepts of programming for Microsoft Office Outlook 2007 using VSTO 3.0 and C#. We will take a look at the following:

- An overview of the Outlook object model and its features in VSTO
- Learning the extensibility of Microsoft Office Outlook 2007 using the object model
- Learning to customize Microsoft Office Outlook menus and toolbars using VSTO
- Working with form regions in Outlook, manipulating folders, contact information, and mail items using VSTO programming
- Learning the concepts and seeing a demonstration of working with Outlook meetings and appointments
- Working with Ribbons for Outlook 2007
- Outlook applications and the Microsoft SQL Server 2008 database interaction

Microsoft Office Outlook object model overview

Programming in Microsoft Office Outlook differs from programming other Microsoft applications such as InfoPath and Excel. Most of the Microsoft Office applications target documents rather than data items, but Microsoft Office Outlook targets each data item stored in the database or the primary data storage used by an Outlook application. Microsoft Office Outlook stores and manages data items such as emails, appointments, notes, tasks, and contacts in tables in a structured database.

The Microsoft Office Outlook object model is based on **COM** (**Component Object Model**) and is used to interact with Outlook form regions, menus, and other application customization possibilities. It is similar to other Microsoft Office application object models when thought of with respect to the object model implementation interfaces for collections, objects, properties, methods, and events.

COM is a language-neutral way of implementing objects that can be used in different environments.

A large numbers of objects are available for developing and customizing Outlook 2007. If the developer needs to develop application add-ins for Outlook, he or she can program using the objects provided by the Outlook object model. In the Outlook object model, the class will represent each object in the UI to the user. For example, the `Microsoft.Office.Interop.Outlook.Application` class represents the entire application, and the `Microsoft.Office.Interop.Outlook.MailItem` class represents an email message.

To get used to the object models in Outlook, you should be familiar with some of the top-level objects. The `Application` object represents an Outlook application, and it is the highest level class in the Outlook object model. The `Explorer` object corresponds to the window that displays the contents of a folder, and contains Outlook data items such as email messages, tasks, appointments, and so on. The `MAPIFolder` object represents the folder that contains emails, contacts, tasks, and other Outlook data items. By default, there are sixteen `MAPIFolder` objects available. The `Inspector` object corresponds to a window that displays a single item such as a particular email message, or a specific contact item.

Let's see how to create application-level add-ins for Microsoft Office Outlook 2007 using VSTO 3.0. We will create a **Hello World** application-level example for Microsoft Office Outlook 2007 using Visual Studio 2008.

1. Open Visual Studio 2008 to create a new **Outlook 2007 Add-in** template project.

2. Select **New Project**. Under **Office** select **2007**, and then select the **Microsoft Outlook Add-in** template, and name the project as per your requirements.

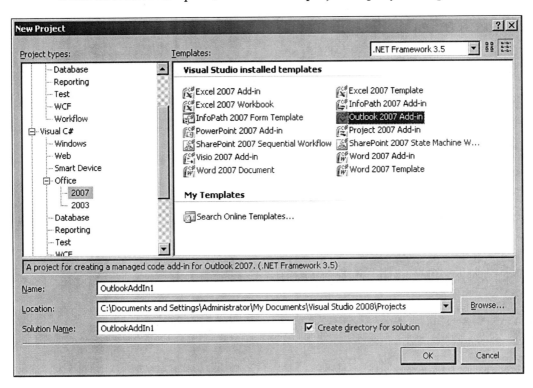

3. The solution will be created with all of the supporting files required for the development of Outlook solution, as shown in the following screenshot:

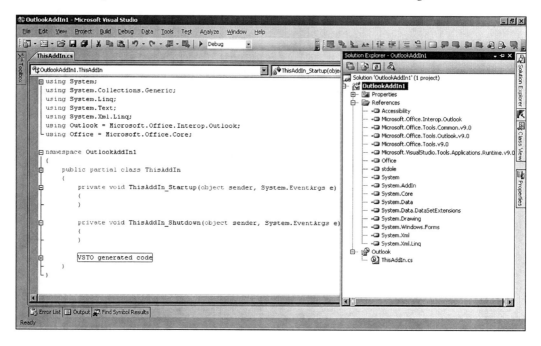

4. Write the following code to display a message box:

```
// Windows forms namespace to display Message box
    using System.Windows.Forms;
```

5. Write the code to display the **Say Hello World!** message while loading:

```
private void ThisAddIn_Startup(object sender, System.EventArgs e)
{
// Message box display
    MessageBox.Show("Say Hello World!");
}
```

The result will be similar to what is shown in the following screenshot:

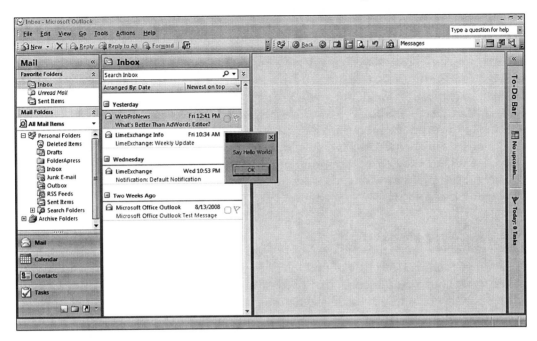

Outlook 2007 object models are categorized and mapped correspondingly. The following Outlook object models hold all of Outlook's objects for programming in their corresponding object model categories: Items object model, Navigation bars and Outlook bars object model, Rules object model, and Views object model. In the Application object model hierarchy, the `Application` object is the parent of all other Outlook objects.

Customization using VSTO

Most enterprise business applications are loaded with a wide variety of features for users. Even though these applications have a wide range of features, many business requirements can be fulfilled only through customization because not all applications are designed to fit each and every enterprise's special needs. Customization for most of the application is a tough job to execute.

Outlook 2007 is loaded with a wide variety of features that will satisfy a broad range of user categories. Some organizations need more functionality and features to be added, so that the application will satisfy their custom business requirements. VSTO 3.0 helps Office developers to customize and enhance the Outlook 2007 application as per the user's business requirements.

Microsoft Office Outlook 2007 supports other Microsoft Office tools such as InfoPath and Excel, in order to provide seamless collaboration.

VSTO provides an easy way to create an application-level add-in for Outlook 2007 using Visual Studio 2008. Creating add-ins for Microsoft Office Outlook 2007 has been more complex to work out, but VSTO 3.0 offers Office developers with project templates in Visual Studio 2008 to allow them to create add-ins for Outlook 2007. Adding to the project templates, VSTO offers great support for development and deployment, which improves the development work. This provides .NET framework support for Outlook 2007 add-in programming, which includes class library support, controlled exception handling, memory management, extensibility, ClickOnce deployment, and so on.

Menus in Outlook

A group of commands or lists of options from which you can choose your desired operation is known as a menu. Most of the latest applications are menu driven. Microsoft Office Outlook, which is a menu-driven application, provides the user with an easy flowing UI for user interaction. Most of the menu-driven applications will provide you with basic customization such as choosing the menu for the default view of the application, and so on.

 In Microsoft Office, all menus and toolbars are CommandBars. A CommandBar is a static collection shared by all Windows. There are standard toolbars, menu bars, context menus, and so on. A small add-in enumerates and displays all Microsoft Outlook CommandBars.

Likewise, Microsoft Office Outlook 2007 provides the option for a user to customize the menus. VSTO 3.0 provides Office developers with the ability to build custom menus and customize the existing menus using the .NET framework and support a programming language. You can even rebuild the classic menu style for Outlook 2007 by using the VSTO 3.0 application level add-ins development.

Let's create a custom menu in the menu bar of the Outlook and add a new item to the menu. This way, you will get to know about custom menu development for Microsoft Office Outlook 2007.

Open Visual Studio 2008 and create a new solution, as described in the previous example.

Let's write a program to create a menu item and call it **Say Hello World**.

```
// Defining new Menubar
    private Office.CommandBar PacktOldMenuBar;
// Defining old Menubar
    private Office.CommandBarPopup PacktNewMenuBar;
// Defining instance of button for menu item
    private Office.CommandBarButton PacktButton1;
// Tag string for our Menu item
    private string strMenuString = "Outlook AddIn #1";

    private void ThisAddIn_Startup(object sender,
        System.EventArgs e)
    {
// Define the Old Menu Bar
        PacktOldMenuBar = this.Application.ActiveExplorer().
            CommandBars.ActiveMenuBar;

// Define the new Menu Bar into the existing menu bar
        PacktNewMenuBar = (Office.CommandBarPopup)PacktOldMenuBar.
            Controls.Add(Office.MsoControlType.msoControlPopup,
                missing, missing, missing, false);

//If PacktNewMenuBar not found then the code will add it
        if (PacktNewMenuBar != null)
        {
// Set caption for the Menu
            PacktNewMenuBar.Caption = "Packt Menu Item 1";

// Tag string value passing
            PacktNewMenuBar.Tag = strMenuString;

// Assigning button type
            PacktButton1 = (Office.
                CommandBarButton)PacktNewMenuBar.
                Controls.Add(Office.MsoControlType.
                msoControlButton, missing, missing, 1, true);

// Setting up the button style
            PacktButton1.Style = Office.MsoButtonStyle.
                msoButtonIconAndCaptionBelow;

// Set button caption
            PacktButton1.Caption = "Say Hello World";

// Set the menu visible
            PacktNewMenuBar.Visible = true;
        }
    }
```

The following screenshot displays the resulting menu developed by you using the preceding code:

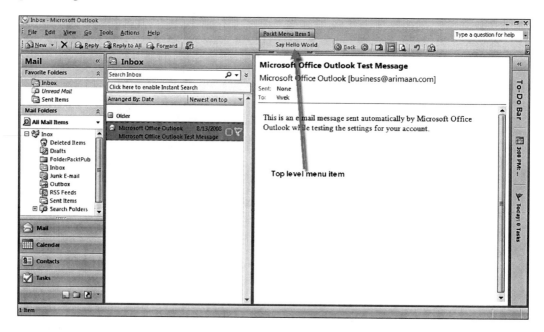

You can also build more custom menus for your Outlook 2007 with functionality as per your requirements. VSTO will speed up development and provide support for a hassle free environment for the developer to work on Outlook 2007 add-ins and other customization.

Toolbars in Outlook

Generally, toolbars provide easy access to the functionality of the application by using buttons and menus. Most application's user interfaces have a toolbar that has buttons, menus, and input or output control elements for user interaction with the application. Even applications allow users to do visual customization of toolbars as per the users' needs.

Microsoft Office Outlook 2007 provides a very good visual representation of toolbars for user interaction with the application. Outlook provides support for toolbar customization to improve custom visual interaction for users. VSTO 3.0 offers wide options to build custom toolbars and to customize existing toolbars as per the user's needs.

Remember that menus and CommandBars are not VSTO features, but
are in the `Microsoft.Office` namespace. VSTO is making it easier to
program for the Office object model.

Let's see a demonstration of creating a custom toolbar with a button.

1. Open Visual Studio 2008, and create a new solution, as described above.
2. Next, add the reference needed to show the message box needed in
    our demonstration:

    ```
    // Namespace reference for message box
        using System.Windows.Forms;
    ```

3. Let's write a program to create a toolbar and call it **Hello World!**.

    ```
    // Declare the toolbar
        Office.CommandBar PacktCustomToolBar;

    // Declare the button
        Office.CommandBarButton PacktButtonA;

    private void ThisAddIn_Startup(object sender, System.EventArgs e)
    {
    // Verify the PacktCustomToolBar exist and add to the application
        if (PacktCustomToolBar == null)
        {
        // Adding the commandbar to Active explorer
            Office.CommandBars PacktBars = this.Application.
                ActiveExplorer().CommandBars;

        // Adding PacktCustomToolBar to the commandbars
            PacktCustomToolBar = PacktBars.Add("NewPacktToolBar",
                Office.MsoBarPosition.msoBarTop, false, true);
        }
    // Adding button to the custom tool bar
        Office.CommandBarButton MyButton1 = (Office.
            CommandBarButton)PacktCustomToolBar.Controls.Add(1,
            missing, missing, missing, missing);
    // Set the button style
        MyButton1.Style = Office.MsoButtonStyle.msoButtonCaption;
    // Set the caption and tag string
        MyButton1.Caption = "PACKT BUTTON";
        MyButton1.Tag = "MY BUTTON";
    ```

```
                    if (this.PacktButtonA == null)
                    {
                    // Adding the event handler for the button in the toolbar
                        this.PacktButtonA = MyButton1;
                        PacktButtonA.Click += new Office.
                            _CommandBarButtonEvents_ClickEventHandler(ButtonClick);
                    }
            }

            // Button event in the custom toolbar
            private void ButtonClick(Office.CommandBarButton ButtonContrl,
                ref bool CancelOption)
            {
            // Message box displayed on button click
                MessageBox.Show(ButtonContrl.Caption + " Says Hello World!");
            }
```

The following image shows the results of adding a custom toolbar with button control:

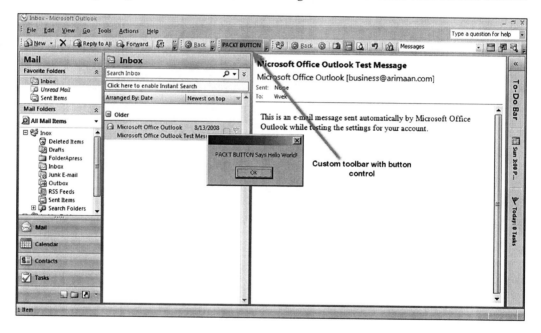

The CommandBars object helps you to build variants of toolbars to your Outlook 2007 application's user interface. Microsoft Office Outlook 2007 is the only tool in the Microsoft Office 2007 family to support both standard toolbars and the new Ribbon in their UI.

Outlook form regions support

Before the release of Microsoft Office Outlook 2007, Outlook forms were the only option for creating a custom UI. In Outlook 2007, you have a new feature called form regions. Form regions are a new way of customizing the Outlook. Form regions are the added feature of the UI in the standard Microsoft Office Outlook 2007. Form regions will add custom functionality–they will build a new range of options in the UI for Microsoft Office Outlook 2007.

When you work with standard forms, you can see that all Outlook items have a MessageClass property that determines the type of objects you're working on, for example, contact, appointment, task, email, post, or journal entry. All of the standard forms are stored in the standard forms library. Form regions are the replacement for the standard forms, to display the custom reading pane, and add new pages to Outlook. In form regions, the controls can be bound to the Outlook properties.

Outlook forms bring you a new design with the support of .NET controls, in order to easily integrate with your Visual Studio Designer and provide code templates and debugging options.

1. Open Visual Studio 2008, to create a new **Outlook 2007 Add-in** template project.

2. Select **New Project**. Under **Office** select **2007** and select **Outlook 2007 Add-in** template and name the project as per your requirement.

3. The solution will be created with all of supporting files required for the development of our Outlook solution.

4. Right-click on your project solution and click on the **Add New Item** option. Select the **Outlook Form Region** template as shown in the following screenshot:

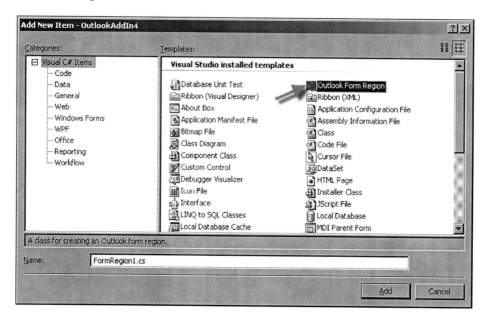

5. After clicking on the **Add** button in the Visual Studio 2008 **Add New Item** dialog box, a wizard window in which you can set the properties for **New Outlook Form Region** will appear as shown in the following screenshot:

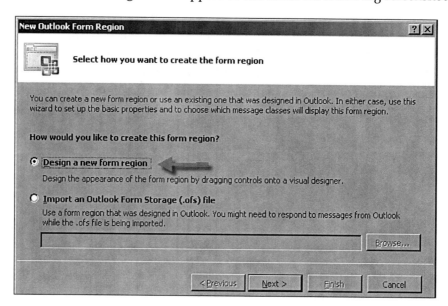

6. A form region can be created as either a separate form or as a form adjoining the existing form, or you can also overwrite an existing form with the new form you're creating. In the **New Outlook Form Region** wizard, you have options to select accordingly.

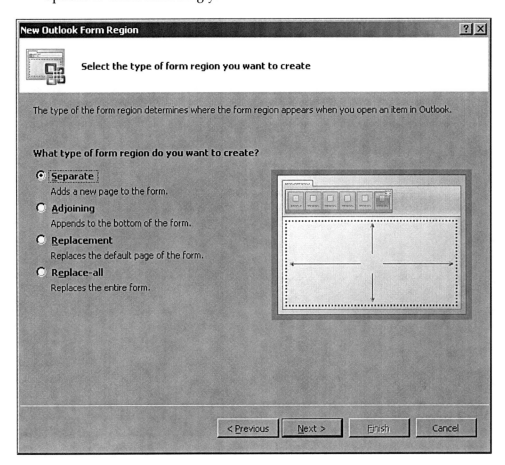

7. Name the new Outlook form region as per your requirements:

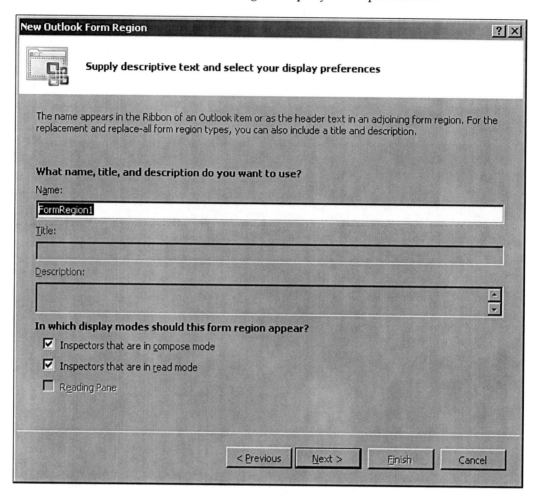

8. Next, associate the standard message classes to the Outlook form region:

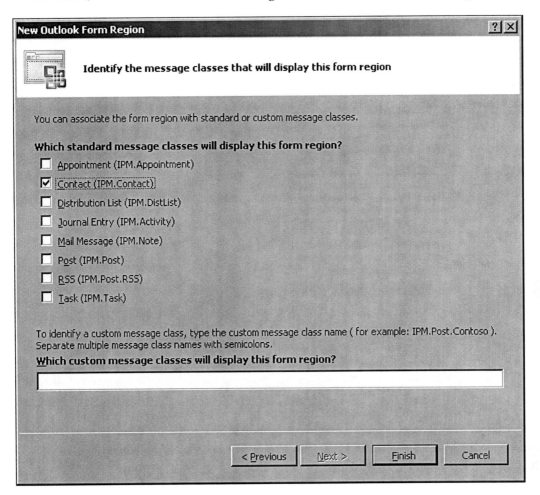

9. Once you are done creating the Outlook form region, run the solution. The new form region will appear as shown in the following screenshot:

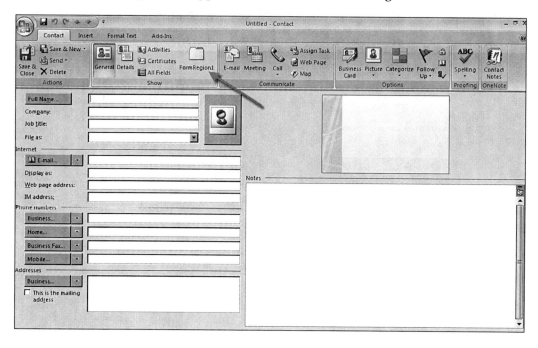

10. We can also write a program to display the current contact item's email address in the form region. Open the `FormRegion1.cs` file and write the following code inside the `FormRegionShowing` event:

```
// Occurs before the form region is displayed
// Use this.OutlookItem to get a reference to the current
    Outlook item
// Use this.OutlookFormRegion to get a reference to the
    form region

private void FormRegion1_FormRegionShowing(object sender,
    System.EventArgs e)
{
// Verify the current Outlook item is Outlook contact item
    if (this.OutlookItem is Outlook.ContactItem)
    {
    // Get reference through the Outlook contact item
        Outlook.ContactItem PacktMailContactItem = (Outlook.
            ContactItem)this.OutlookItem;

    // Message box displayed while you click the form region
        button in the Ribbon
```

```
        MessageBox.Show("This form region to display: " +
            PacktMailContactItem.Email1DisplayName);
    // The listview control displays the current contacts
        display email
        ContactListView.Items.Add(PacktMailContactItem.
            Email1DisplayName.ToString());
    }
}
```

The addition and execution of the preceding code results in the following screenshot:

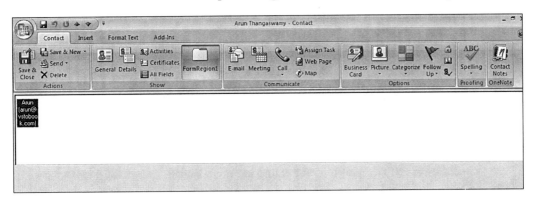

One of the key advantages of form regions is that you can use themed controls that match the look of standard Outlook forms in Outlook 2007, and you also have easy access to new controls for date and time picking, and time zones. Form regions will help you to build custom contact forms, meeting invitees, and enhanced UI for Microsoft Office Outlook 2007. Outlook 2007 also contains a huge number of new form controls that offer the business logic and performance that users expect from Outlook forms.

Manipulation

Manipulation is an essential element for the efficient development of a reliable solution to satisfy any kind of business need. Manipulation plays the most important role in customization and development of any kind of solution for mature enterprise applications. The primary part of manipulation is the data. Microsoft Office Outlook 2007 allows a wide range of data item manipulation methods inside the application — you can manipulate mail items, contact items, folders in Outlook, and so on. Let's see some examples of manipulation.

Folders

Folders are the containers that hold file items and sub folders inside the main folder. Folders are used to manage mail items to make them easily accessible inside Outlook. In Outlook 2007, you can manage mail items, contact items, and other communication information.

Let's start working with the Outlook folder using VSTO 3.0 and C#.NET programming. The following code will create a folder with your desired name, by using VSTO object models.

1. Open Visual Studio 2008 to create a new **Outlook 2007 Add-in** template project.

2. Select **New Project**. Under **Office** select **2007**, and then select **Outlook 2007 Add-in** template and name the project as per your requirement.

3. The solution will be created with all of the supporting files required for the development of our Outlook solution.

4. Enter the following code, which will dynamically create a folder, inside the ThisAddIn.cs file:

```csharp
private void ThisAddIn_Startup(object sender, System.EventArgs e)
{
// Get the namespace for Outlook operation
    Outlook.NameSpace ReadOutLookNameSpace = this.Application.
        GetNamespace("MAPI");

// Get the default folder names from the Outlook
    Outlook.MAPIFolder ReadDefaultFolders = ReadOutLookNameSpace.
        GetDefaultFolder(Outlook.OlDefaultFolders.olFolderInbox);

// Create folder in the "FolderPacktPub"
    ReadDefaultFolders = this.Application.Session.Folders[1].
        Folders.Add("FolderPacktPub", missing);
}
```

We can see the dynamically-created folder named **FolderPacktPub o**n the leftmost side of the Outlook screen, as shown in the following screenshot:

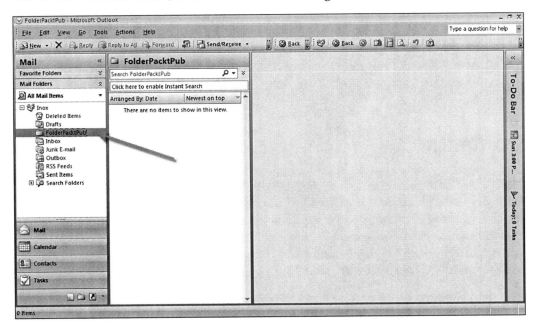

The folders contain **Items** collections which hold items that are compatible with the type of data that is supported in Microsoft Office Outlook 2007. The `GetDefaultFolder()` method is used to retrieve a reference to the **Sent Items** folder. This is declared in order to get default folders by using new `Folder` objects for Outlook 2007.

You may need to clean up Outlook by deleting unwanted folders. The delete operation for folders inside Outlook can be performed by using the `MAPIFolder` object and the properties and methods exposed by the object. Let's see an example of how to delete a folder using the VSTO object. In this example, you are going to run the operation at the initialization of the add-in. You can do the same thing by using the `Click` event for the button that was placed on the toolbar (or anywhere else you need).

Open Visual Studio 2008 and create a new solution, as explained earlier. Write the following code, which will dynamically delete a folder in the `ThisAddIn.cs` file:

```
private void ThisAddIn_Startup(object sender, System.EventArgs e)
{
// Loading the NameSpace needed to manipulate MAPI
    Outlook.NameSpace PacktNameSpace = this.Application.
        GetNamespace("MAPI");
// Accessing the folder through MAPIFolder Object
```

```
// PacktNameSpace.Folders is a collection of all the folders
// We want to delete the 13th folder, FolderPackt
    Outlook.MAPIFolder PacktFolders = PacktNameSpace.Folders[13];
// Getting the folder named FolderPackt
    PacktFolders.Name = "FolderPackt";
// Doing the delete operation using Delete method
    PacktFolders.Delete();
}
```

Contacts

Contacts contain information about communication with a person. The information can be their address, name, phone number, and other relevant information. The **Contacts** folder in Microsoft Office Outlook 2007 is the electronic form of managing contact information about people. Outlook offers the ability to very easily manage multiple phone numbers and more information for a single person. Outlook provides better management of contact entries and brings easy access through the information available in the **Contacts** folder.

In certain situations, you may need to add or modify the contact entries dynamically. To support these features, Microsoft provides a solution through VSTO 3.0 programming to allow Office developers to build application-level add-ins, which will help you integrate custom developed solutions.

We will now create a contact item using the VSTO 3.0 object model and C#.

Open Visual Studio 2008 and create a new solution, as explained earlier. Write the following code, which will dynamically create a contact item in the `ThisAddIn.cs` file.

```
private void ThisAddIn_Startup(object sender, System.EventArgs e)
{
// Using the Outlook object reading through the contact item
    folders
// Preparing to create a new contact item
    Outlook.ContactItem OutlookPacktContact = (Outlook.
        ContactItem)this.Application.CreateItem(Outlook.
        OlItemType.olContactItem);
// Set FirstName property
    OutlookPacktContact.FirstName = "Radhika";
// Set LastName property
    OutlookPacktContact.LastName = "Rajagopalan";
// Set Email1Address property
```

```
    OutlookPacktContact.Email1Address = "radhika@vsto.com";
// Set CompanyName property
    OutlookPacktContact.CompanyName = "ACC Inc";

// Set Categories property
    OutlookPacktContact.Categories = "Packt Group";

// Now save the above contact item
    OutlookPacktContact.Save();
}
```

After executing the source code, you will get the following screenshot as the output for your solution.

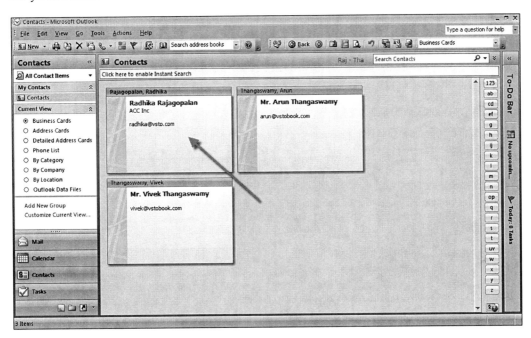

`ContactItem` is the object used to access the contact in a **Contacts** folder by using Outlook programming. The `ContactItem` object has been exposed with a wide variety of properties, events, and methods to program for the **Contact** folder in Outlook 2007.

You have seen how to create a new contact item by using an object in Outlook 2007. Let's take a look at one of the most important contact management features in Microsoft Office Outlook: the distribution list. A distribution list is a collection of email contact information that has been grouped into a single list. VSTO helps Office developers create and modify distribution lists by using the `DistListItem` object.

Let's create a distribution list dynamically, using the VSTO Outlook object model and C# programming.

Open Visual Studio 2008 and create a new solution, as described earlier. Write the following code, which will dynamically create a distribution list, inside the `ThisAddIn.cs` file:

```
private void ThisAddIn_Startup(object sender, System.EventArgs e)
{
// Using the Outlook object reading through the Distribution item
// Preparing to create a new Distribution item
    Outlook.DistListItem OutlookPacktDistributionList = (Outlook.
        DistListItem)this.Application.CreateItem(Outlook.OlItemType.
        olDistributionListItem);
// Name the new distribution list
    OutlookPacktDistributionList.DLName = "PacktContactList";
// To set the recipient information, create the mailitem
    collect object
    Outlook.MailItem PacktListItem = (Outlook.MailItem)this.
        Application.CreateItem(Outlook.OlItemType.olMailItem);
// Adding mail items
    PacktListItem.Recipients.Add("Radhika Rajagopalan
        <radhika@bookvsto.com>");
    PacktListItem.Recipients.Add("Vivek Thangaswamy
        <vivek@bookvsto.com>");
// Adding the recipients to the new distribution
    OutlookPacktDistributionList.AddMembers(PacktListItem.Recipients);
// Save the new distribution using Save method
    OutlookPacktDistributionList.Save();
}
```

The newly-distribution list appears as shown in the following screenshot:

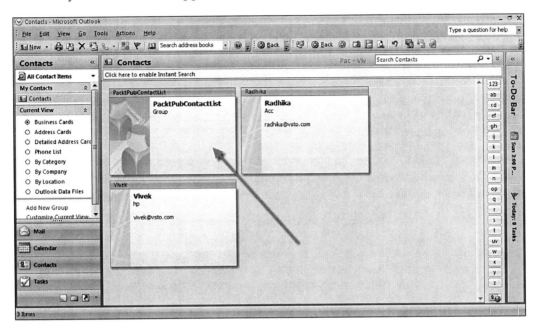

On clicking the **Members** tab in the solution, we get a list of the recipients, or members, as shown in the following screenshot:

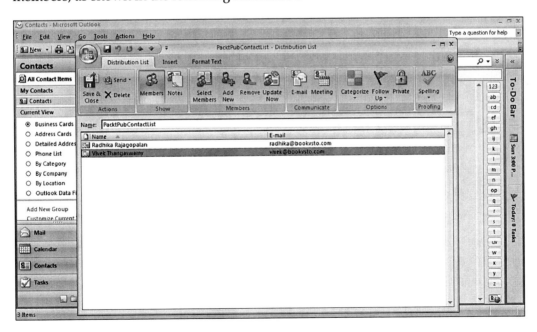

Email messages

Email is an electronic form of storing information that can be shared with people via an electronic communication system. You can write, send, and receive information without using paper, and communicate through electronic systems by using a digital copy of the information.

You can do many email operations through VSTO programming, such as composing mail items at runtime using Office objects. Let's create a new mail that has a **Subject**, **To**, **Address** and few other properties, by using the VSTO Outlook MailItem object.

Open Visual Studio 2008 and create a new solution, as explained earlier. Write the following code, which will dynamically create a mail item, inside the ThisAddIn.cs file:

```
private void ThisAddIn_Startup(object sender, System.EventArgs e)
{
// Outlook mailitem object to compose new mail
    Outlook.MailItem PacktMailItem = (Outlook.MailItem)this.
        Application.CreateItem(Outlook.OlItemType.olMailItem);
// Set the To address property value
    PacktMailItem.To = "radhika@vsto.com";
// Set the Subject property value
    PacktMailItem.Subject = "Mail from PacktPub Editor";
// Set the Body property value
    PacktMailItem.Body = "Your book is ready to buy!";
// Set the Importance level for the mail
    PacktMailItem.Importance = Outlook.OlImportance.
        olImportanceNormal;
// If parameter is set to false compose mail won't display
    PacktMailItem.Display(true);
// To send the composed mailitem
// ((Outlook._MailItem) PacktMailItem).Send();
}
```

The results of the execution of the preceding code example can be seen in the following screenshot:

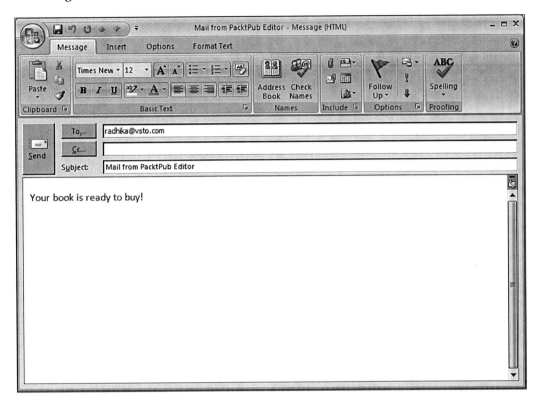

The `Microsoft.Office.Interop.Outlook.MailItem` class represents an email message. `MailItem` objects are usually found in folders, such as **Inbox**, **Sent Items**, and **Outbox**. The `MailItem` exposes properties and methods that can be used to create and send email messages.

With Outlook 2007 mail items, you have the option to categorize mail using colors. This categorization can be achieved by the use of VSTO objects. Mail items can be categorized programmatically. `Outlook.MailItem` is the object used to access mail items in Outlook 2007.

The following image is a typical view of the category option available in Outlook 2007:

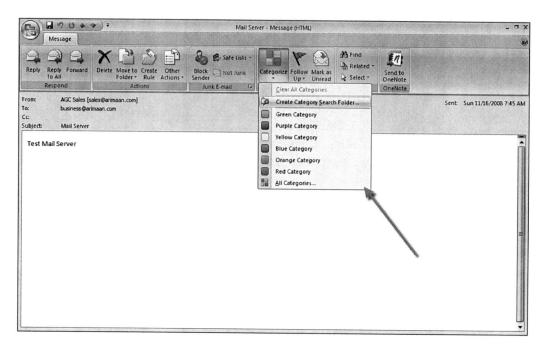

Let's see in an example of how to get the category property by using the VSTO objects for the mail items.

Open Visual Studio 2008 and create a new solution, as described earlier. Write the following code to the context menu item in the mail box folder, inside the ThisAddIn.cs file:

```
private void ThisAddIn_Startup(object sender, System.EventArgs e)
{
// Creates a new mail item instance
    Outlook.MailItem OLmailitems = (Outlook.MailItem)this.Application.
        CreateItem(OlItemType.olMailItem);
// Get the category dialog window for the mail items
    OLmailitems.ShowCategoriesDialog();
}
```

After executing this program, we can see the different color properties, as shown in the following screenshot:

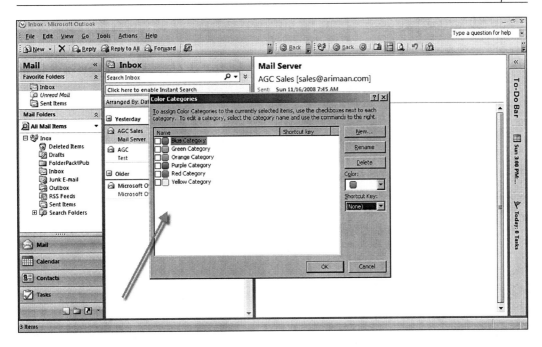

VSTO also supports the customization of Outlook 2007 context menu items. Let's look at an example to add a custom menu item in the context menu item of the email folder in Outlook.

Open Visual Studio 2008 and create a new solution, as explained earlier. Write the following code to the context menu item in the mail box folder, inside the `ThisAddIn.cs` file:

```
private void ThisAddIn_Startup(object sender, System.EventArgs e)
{
// Custom context menu item event managed
    this.Application.ItemContextMenuDisplay += new Microsoft.Office.
        Interop.Outlook.ApplicationEvents_11_
        ItemContextMenuDisplayEventHandler(
        PacktMenuItem_ItemContextMenuDisplay);
}

// Context menu item adding procedure
public void PacktMenuItem_ItemContextMenuDisplay(Microsoft.Office.
    Core.CommandBar PacktCommandBar, Microsoft.Office.Interop.Outlook.
    Selection Selection)
{
// Commadbarpopup control to context menu item
```

```
Office.CommandBarPopup PacktCustomItem =
    (Office.CommandBarPopup) PacktCommandBar.Controls.Add(Office.
    MsoControlType.msoControlPopup, Type.Missing,
    "Custom Menu Item", PacktCommandBar.Controls.Count + 1,
    Type.Missing);
// Added to separate group in context menu
    PacktCustomItem.BeginGroup = true;

// Set the tag value for the menu
    PacktCustomItem.Tag = "PacktCustomMenuItem";

// Caption for the context menu item
    PacktCustomItem.Caption = "Custom Menu Item1";

// Set it to visible
    PacktCustomItem.Visible = true;
}
```

The resulting custom menu item in the **Inbox** mail folder is visible in the following screenshot:

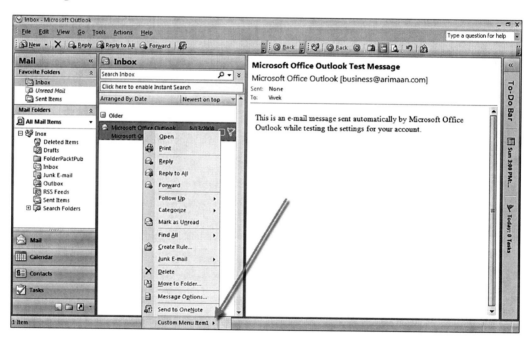

Working with Appointments

Before I explain the Appointments feature in Microsoft Office Outlook 2007, let me explain the Microsoft Office Outlook calendar. This will help you understand the concepts of Appointments more easily, and also explain how you can utilize this functionality for your needs. The Microsoft Outlook 2007 calendar is the scheduling component of the Outlook mail management system. It is well-integrated with other Microsoft Outlook functionality such as email, contacts, appointments, and other items in.

Appointments are the actions you're scheduling in your Outlook calendar, inviting other people to participate if required. You can set the status of your availability for an appointment, and you can also schedule recurring appointments.

Let's create an Outlook Appointment dynamically by using VSTO objects and C# programming:

Open Visual Studio 2008 and create a new solution, as described earlier. Write the following code, which will dynamically create an Appointment item in the `ThisAddIn.cs` file:

```
private void ThisAddIn_Startup(object sender, System.EventArgs e)
{
// Outlook AppointmentItem object to compose new Appointment
    Outlook.AppointmentItem PacktAppointmentItem = (Outlook.
        AppointmentItem)this.Application.CreateItem(Outlook.
        OlItemType.olAppointmentItem);
// Set the subject property value
    PacktAppointmentItem.Subject = "Regarding book review";
// Set the location property value
    PacktAppointmentItem.Location = "Meeting Hall";
// Set the start date
    PacktAppointmentItem.Start = DateTime.Today;
// Set the end date
    PacktAppointmentItem.End = DateTime.Today;
// Set the body property value
    PacktAppointmentItem.Body = "Book review comments from
        all editors";
// Set the required attendee information
    PacktAppointmentItem.RequiredAttendees = "vivek@vsto.com";
// Set the optional attandee information
    PacktAppointmentItem.OptionalAttendees = "radhika@vsto.com";
// If parameter is set to false compose Appointment won't display
    PacktAppointmentItem.Display(true);
// To send the composed PacktAppointmentItem
//((Outlook._AppointmentItem)PacktAppointmentItem).Send();
}
```

The following screenshot shows the results of adding and executing this code:

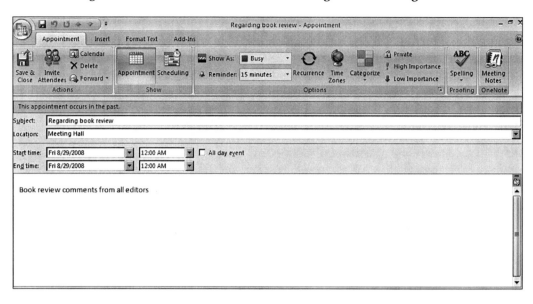

The `AppointmentItem` object is used to create appointments dynamically. An `AppointmentItem` object can be used to create a meeting, a one-time appointment, or a recurring appointment.

Let's perform a demonstration of how to delete a recurring appointment from your Outlook 2007 calendar, by using VSTO programming.

Open Visual Studio 2008 and create a new solution, as described earlier. Write the following code, which will dynamically delete an Appointment item, inside the `ThisAddIn.cs` file:

```
private void ThisAddIn_Startup(object sender, System.EventArgs e)
{
// Reading the calendar folder through MEPIFolder object
    Outlook.MAPIFolder PacktCalendarInfo = Application.Session.
        GetDefaultFolder(Outlook.OlDefaultFolders.
            olFolderCalendar);
// Get the data items in the calendar folder
    Outlook.Items PacktCalendarDataItems = PacktCalendarInfo.Items;
// Searching the Appointment items based on subject
    Outlook.AppointmentItem PacktAppointmentItem =
        PacktCalendarDataItems["Book release"] as Outlook.
        AppointmentItem;
```

```
// Selected appointment's recurrence information
   Outlook.RecurrencePattern PacktRecPattern = PacktAppointmentItem.
      GetRecurrencePattern();

// Loading the appointment to AppointmentItem Object
   Outlook.AppointmentItem PacktAppointmentDelete = PacktRecPattern.
      GetOccurrence(new DateTime(2008, 9, 28, 8, 0, 0));

// Now delete using the Delete method
   PacktAppointmentDelete.Delete();
}
```

Working with meetings

Meetings are generally discussions amongst more than two people, during which predetermined topics are discussed. Meetings help you prepare a plan, or finalize pending work, or perform other tasks involving colleagues. In Microsoft Office Outlook, a meeting is a scheduled appointment—that is, people are invited to attend. You can set the meeting time and other options for the meeting attendees, to process the invitation.

VSTO 3.0 supports the dynamic creation of meeting items for Office. Let's create a meeting invitation dynamically, by using the VSTO object model and C# programming.

Open Visual Studio 2008 and create a new solution, as explained earlier. Write the following code, which will dynamically create a meeting invite item, inside the `ThisAddIn.cs` file:

```
private void ThisAddIn_Startup(object sender, System.EventArgs e)
{
// Outlook PacktMeetingItem object to compose new meeting request
   Outlook.AppointmentItem PacktMeetingItem = (Outlook.
      AppointmentItem)this.Application.CreateItem(Microsoft.Office.
      Interop.Outlook.OlItemType.olAppointmentItem);

   PacktMeetingItem.MeetingStatus = Microsoft.Office.
      Interop.Outlook.OlMeetingStatus.olMeeting;

// Set the subject for the meeting
   PacktMeetingItem.Subject = "Changes in book content";

// Update the body information of the meeting
   PacktMeetingItem.Body = "Work on the changes and update";

// Start Expiry Time of the meeting
   PacktMeetingItem.Start = new DateTime(2008, 9, 28, 9, 0, 0);
```

```
      // Set the recipient information
         Outlook.Recipient PacktRecipient = PacktMeetingItem.Recipients.
            Add("Radhika Rajagopalan");

         PacktRecipient.Type = (int)Outlook.OlMeetingRecipientType.
            olRequired;

      // If parameter is set to false compose MeetingItem won't display
         PacktMeetingItem.Display(true);

      // To send the composed PacktMeetingItem
      //((Outlook.MeetingItem)PacktMeetingItem).Send();
      }
```

As we can see in the following screenshot, a **Meeting** tab is created successfully after executing this program.

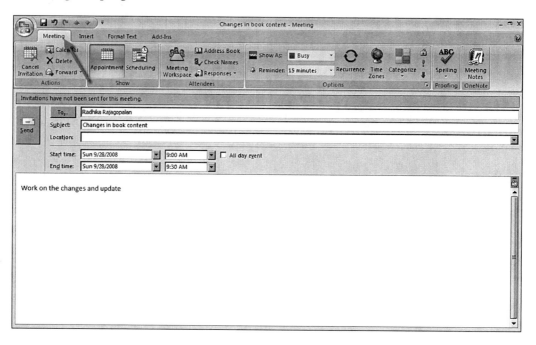

An Outlook meeting is one of the many types of Appointments in Outlook. Meetings are internally linked with the Outlook calendar. A meeting request can be created using only the AppointmentItem object. To create and set the meeting invitation by using the AppointmentItem, you must set the MeetingStatus property to olMeeting.

Creating a Ribbon menu for Outlook 2007

The Ribbon is the new way of presenting menus for Office users and organizing related commands; visually it will appear as controls. The Ribbon menu feature is supported in most of the Office 2007 applications, such as Word, Excel, and Outlook. InfoPath and Visio are not provided with the Ribbon menu feature.

Let's create a Ribbon menu for Outlook by using Outlook objects and Visual designer support. In this example, we will create a Ribbon menu with a button on it. When you click the button, the option for composing a new mail will open.

1. Open Visual Studio 2008 and create a new solution, as described earlier.

2. Next, let's add the Ribbon component to our solution. Right-click on the project, and select **Add | New Item... | Ribbon (Visual Designer)**, from the context menu. Name the Ribbon component as `Ribbon1.cs`, and click **OK**.

 Ribbon Visual Designer is a control that provides a visual designer for basic Ribbon customization tasks.

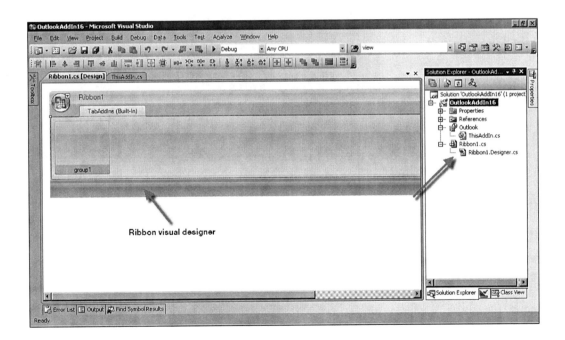

3. Expand the **Toolbox** sliding window in Visual Studio 2008, and you can find the controls that support the Ribbon menu under Office customization.

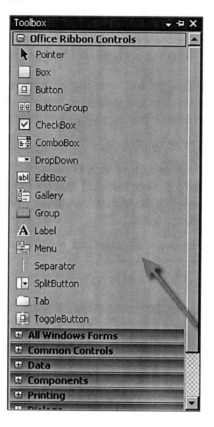

4. Next, drag-and-drop the controls that are required for your development inside your group control in the Ribbon. In this example, you are going to use the Button control.

5. The Outlook Ribbon menu is quite different from other Office applications. The Ribbon menu varies for each Outlook region. For example, for reading a mail, you will see different Ribbon menu commands to those for an appointment and so on. To view your add-in that has the Ribbon menu, you need to specify the Ribbon types.

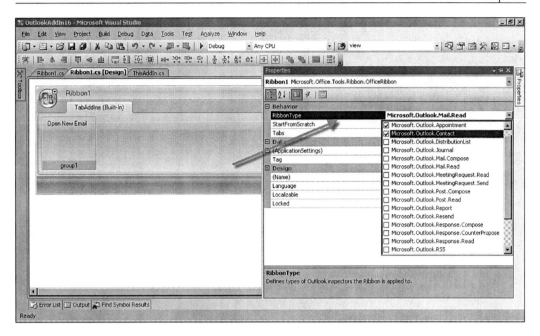

6. To create a program that will open a window for composing a new mail on
    a button click event, write the following code snippet inside the Ribbon1.cs
    file. Also include the code using Microsoft.Office.Interop.Outlook; in
    the Ribbon1.cs file to get access to the Outlook objects.

```
// Click event of the button
private void Button_OpenNewMail_Click(object sender,
    RibbonControlEventArgs e)
{
// Application class to get Outlook object references
    ApplicationClass PacktApplication = new ApplicationClass();

// Get the MAPIFolder NameSpaces
    NameSpace PacktNameSpace = PacktApplication.
        GetNamespace("MAPIFolder");

// Access to the default folders
    MAPIFolder ApreeMAPI = PacktNameSpace.
        GetDefaultFolder(OlDefaultFolders.olFolderInbox);

// Outlook mailitem object to compose new mail
    MailItem PacktMailItem = (MailItem)ApreeMAPI.Items.
        Add(OlItemType.olMailItem);

// To display the new mail compose window
    PacktMailItem.Display(true);
}
```

Adding and executing the preceding code results in the following output:

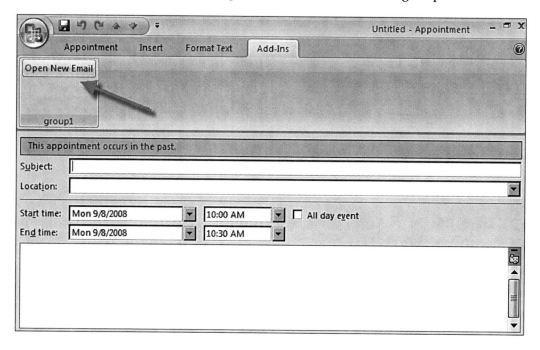

Outlook 2007 data interaction with Microsoft SQL Server 2008

Microsoft presents a programming interface for synchronizing data from an external data source with the Outlook data file dedicated to storing data from that source. As you know, VSTO 3.0 is powerful enough to use features of the .NET technology. Linking the Outlook contacts in a Microsoft SQL Server 2008 database is one of the key features available for Outlook users. Working with your Outlook contacts in a database will keep you informed of changes to Outlook contacts and vice versa.

Let's see how to make your Outlook 2007 application interact with a relational database management system, for example, Microsoft SQL Server 2008. Let's consider a scenario where you want to import all of the contact information for your friends or colleagues that is currently managed in a Microsoft SQL Server 2008 database.

1. Open Visual Studio 2008 and create a new solution, as described earlier.
2. You need to know about the database, and the details of the tables that you are going to import into your contact folder. You can see the table information that is used in this demonstration in the following images:

	ContactID	FirstName	Email	Location	Company
	1	Radhika	radhika@vsto.com	Chennai	Acc
	2	Vivek	vivek@vsto.com	Chennai	hp
▶*	NULL	NULL	NULL	NULL	NULL

3. Let's write a program to establish effective communication with the Microsoft SQL Server 2008 database table, and import the information to Outlook 2007's contact folder, by using the C# programming language and VSTO.

```csharp
private void ThisAddIn_Startup(object sender, System.EventArgs e)
{
// Instantiated datatable, used to read the loaded data
    DataTable PacktDataTable = new DataTable();

// Opening SQL connection for Microsoft SQL Server 2008
    SqlConnection PacktSQLConnection = new SqlConnection(@"Data
        Source=WINNER;Initial Catalog=PacktPub;Integrated
        Security=True");

// Passing SQL command text and SQL connection information

    SqlCommand PacktSQLCommand = new SqlCommand("SELECT * FROM
        Contacts", PacktSQLConnection);

// Open the SQL connection through Open method
    PacktSQLConnection.Open();

// SQL reader to read through data from Database
    SqlDataReader PacktSQLReader = PacktSQLCommand.
        ExecuteReader(CommandBehavior.CloseConnection);

// Load the read data to datatable
    PacktDataTable.Load(PacktSQLReader);

// Now close the datareader
    PacktSQLReader.Close();

// Get the contact folder loaded using MAPIFolder object
```

```csharp
        Outlook.MAPIFolder PacktContactFolder = Application.Session.
            GetDefaultFolder(Outlook.OlDefaultFolders.
            olFolderContacts);
// Accessing the Contact data items through Outlook item object
        Outlook.Items PacktContactItems = PacktContactFolder.Items.
            Restrict("[MessageClass]='IPM.Contact'");
// To read the data one by one from the datatable
        foreach (System.Data.DataRow PacktDataRow in PacktDataTable.
            Rows)
        {
// Check if the current contact item exists in Outlook or not.
            Outlook.ContactItem PacktExistingContact = (Outlook.
                ContactItem)PacktContactItems.Find("[Email1Address] =
                '" + PacktDataRow["Email"] + "'");
// If it exists, then delete
            if (PacktExistingContact != null)
            {
                PacktExistingContact.Delete();
            }
            else
            {
// Create a new contact object and update with data
                from database
                Outlook.ContactItem PacktAddContact = Application.
                    CreateItem(Outlook.OlItemType.olContactItem) as
                    Outlook.ContactItem;
// Assign the value from datarow value
                PacktAddContact.FirstName = PacktDataRow["FirstName"].
                    ToString();

                PacktAddContact.Email1Address = PacktDataRow["Email"].
                    ToString();

                PacktAddContact.CompanyName = PacktDataRow["Company"].
                    ToString();
// Save the assigned values as contact
                PacktAddContact.Save();
            }
        }
    }
```

Once executed, the information stored in the database is retrieved and displayed in the **Contacts** plane, as shown in the following screenshot:

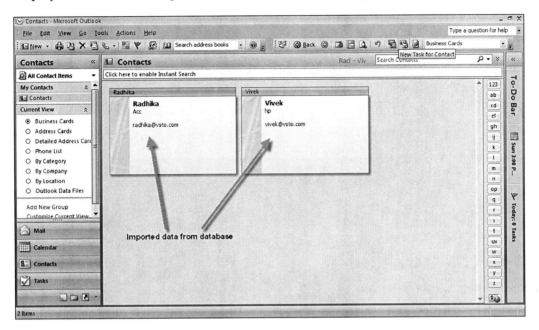

Summary

This chapter examined some important topics regarding programming using VSTO and C# for Microsoft Office Outlook 2007. You have seen the Outlook object model, and how it is used for Outlook application development and customization. This chapter covered the concepts of customizing the Outlook toolbar and menu bar using VSTO. You have learned about VSTO programming support for Outlook form regions. You have seen the most important part of Outlook data manipulation such as email, contacts, and folder manipulation. In the later part of this chapter, you learned programming for a meeting and an appointment in Outlook. You have learned about the Ribbon, and how you can create Ribbons for Outlook. You also learned the concept of database interaction with an Outlook application, with the help of an example of how to connect to a database and get information from it into the **Contact** folder of Outlook. You have seen code examples for each topic, which will make it easier for you to understand the concepts.

6

Microsoft Office PowerPoint, Visio, and Project Programming

Microsoft PowerPoint is a presentation program developed and released by Microsoft Corporation. Microsoft PowerPoint 2007 is a part of the Microsoft Office 2007 suite. Microsoft PowerPoint 2007 is loaded with a wide range of features for its users. VSTO 3.0 helps you to develop application-level solutions for Microsoft PowerPoint 2007. Visual Studio 2008 and VSTO 3.0 provide support for developing application-level add-ins and custom Ribbon development for PowerPoint.

In this chapter, we'll discuss:

- PowerPoint 2007 object model concepts
- Programming in PowerPoint using VSTO 3.0
- Creating a presentation and adding slides using VSTO 3.0
- Visio 2007 Object model concepts
- Programming in Visio using VSTO 3.0
- Shapes and how to manipulate them using VSTO and C# programming
- Working with command bars and document themes
- Programming in Project 2007 using VSTO 3.0
- The concept of the Ribbon, and the introduction of the Visual Designer for the Ribbon
- Creating and customizing Ribbons for PowerPoint 2007

Microsoft Visio is a diagramming software application from Microsoft Corporation. Microsoft Visio 2007 is used for creating vector graphics diagrams. VSTO offers a wide range of objects and classes for developing application-level solutions for Microsoft Visio 2007. VSTO provides full support for custom development of Visio, working with shapes in Visio, customization of toolbars, managing documents, and so on.

Microsoft Project is a project scheduling and controlling tool, developed and released by Microsoft Corporation. Microsoft Project 2007 is designed to support project managers in developing project plans, assigning tasks for resources, tracking project and task progress, managing budgets, and analyzing resources workloads. Microsoft Project is one of the complete project management applications available. VSTO 3.0 provides full support for developing application-level solutions for Microsoft Project. VSTO exposes a wide range of classes, objects, and properties that can be used to customize Microsoft Project 2007.

Programming PowerPoint 2007

VSTO 3.0 provides enhanced support for PowerPoint 2007 to satisfy a user's needs. Currently, VSTO 3.0 supports only application-level customization for Microsoft Office PowerPoint 2007.

Let's consider the following scenario—Zack wants to say hello to all of the PowerPoint 2007 users in the office, and Zack is interested in doing this by using VSTO and Visual Studio 2008. The following example demonstrates, how Zack said hello to all of the PowerPoint 2007 users by using VSTO programming.

Let's see how to create the solution for Microsoft Office PowerPoint 2007 using Visual Studio 2008 and write a **Hello** program as your first programming example, using VSTO 3.0 for Microsoft PowerPoint 2007.

1. Open Visual Studio 2008, to create a new **PowerPoint 2007 Add-in** template project.

2. Select **New Project**. Under **Office** select **2007**, and then select the **Microsoft PowerPoint Add-in** template, and name the project as per your requirements.

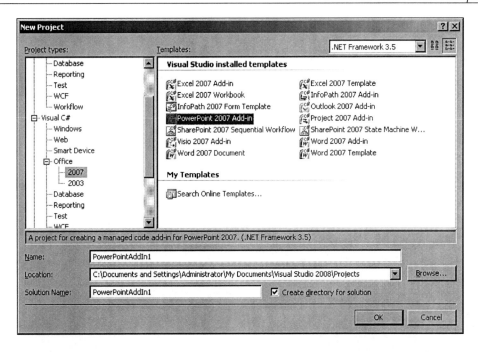

3. The solution will be created with all of the supporting files required for the development of our PowerPoint solution.

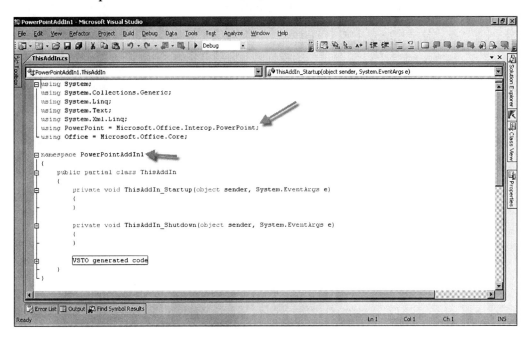

4. Enter using System.Windows.Forms; as the namespace for the message box feature.

5. In the ThisAddIn.cs file, write the following code to say **Hello** to all the Microsoft Office PowerPoint users:

```
private void ThisAddIn_Startup(object sender, System.EventArgs e)
{
// Message box to display information from PowerPoint
    MessageBox.Show("Say Hello! to PowerPoint Users");
}
```

The results of executing this simple program can be seen in the following screenshot:

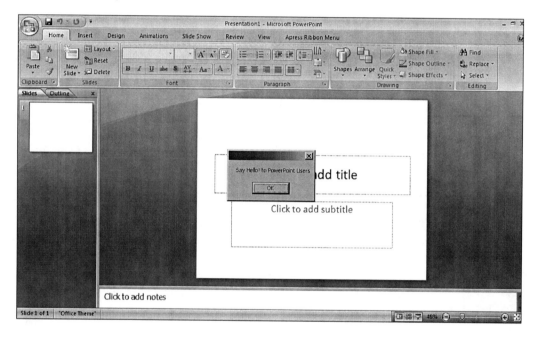

PowerPoint 2007 object model

The object models available in VSTO help PowerPoint Office developers to program against the existing functionality. At first glance, the object models may give the impression of being difficult to understand. On the contrary, it is one of the easiest ways to conceptualize PowerPoint 2007 programming. The object model is a visualization of how every object in PowerPoint is related to the properties of objects. By accessing the objects through the commands, you can manipulate these with VSTO code, programmatically.

VSTO provides you with the finest options for customizing Microsoft Office PowerPoint 2007, which macros don't have. A macro is a series of commands that are executed in sequence. Macros are programmed using **Visual Basic Script (VBScript)**, and are vulnerable to security. VSTO provides full support for C# or VB.NET, the programming languages supported by the .NET framework.

Creating a presentation at runtime

The VSTO 3.0 project template automatically loads the entire alias to your Microsoft Office PowerPoint solution. You can easily reference this through the namespaces and classes available, in order to to build your custom solution for PowerPoint 2007.

Now, let's see how to create a PowerPoint presentation at runtime, using VSTO 3.0 for Microsoft PowerPoint 2007.

Open Visual Studio 2008 and create a new solution. Refer to the previous example for complete instructions on how to do this. Write the following code to create a presentation in Microsoft Office PowerPoint 2007 in the `ThisAddIn.cs` file:

```
private void ThisAddIn_Startup(object sender, System.EventArgs e)
    {
    // Creating PowerPoint presentation with single slide in it
    // Using the PowerPoint object instance adding the
    // Slide with text title structure to the current Presentation
        PowerPoint.Presentation PacktPresentation = this.Application.
            Presentations.Add(Microsoft.Office.Core.MsoTriState.
            msoTriStateMixed);
    }
```

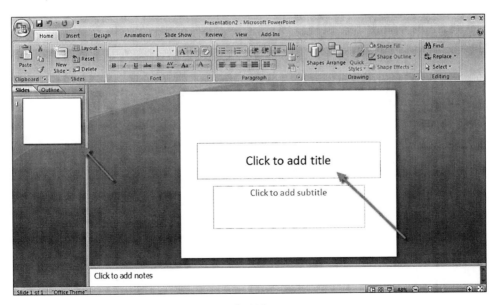

Dynamically add a slide and set title text in the presentation

The VSTO application-level add-in is slightly different for Microsoft Office PowerPoint 2007. VSTO in PowerPoint doesn't have the ability to recognize the default presentation during the startup procedure. This is not a limitation of VSTO in PowerPoint; it is the default behavior of VSTO programming for PowerPoint 2007.

Zack has another task at hand—to create a presentation using PowerPoint 2007, where the presentation should be loaded with a slide and have some text added to it by default. Knowing the default behavior of the VSTO application level add-in for PowerPoint 2007, Zack came up with a solution for this scenario.

VSTO exposes many objects, classes, and events for PowerPoint 2007 programming. Using events exposed by VSTO, you can achieve the solution for this scenario. Zack used the AfterNewPresentation event and developed a solution for it. Let's follow up the procedure and learn how to create a presentation and add a slide to it with text content.

Open Visual Studio 2008 and create a new solution, as described earlier. In the ThisAddIn.cs file, write the following program to add a title slide to the presentation in Microsoft Office PowerPoint 2007:

```
// PowerPoint application object instance
   PowerPoint.Application PacktPowerPointApplication;

   private void ThisAddIn_Startup(object sender, System.EventArgs e)
   {
   // Get access to the instance of current application
      PacktPowerPointApplication = this.Application;

   // Registering the AfterNewPresentation event of the PowerPoint
      PacktPowerPointApplication.AfterNewPresentation +=
          new PowerPoint.EApplication_
          AfterNewPresentationEventHandler(
          PacktPowerPointApplication_AfterNewPresentation);
   }
// AfterNewPresentation event of PowerPoint presentation
   private void PacktPowerPointApplication_AfterNewPresentation(
       PowerPoint.Presentation PacktPresentation)
   {
   // Call the custom function to add slide with text on it
       Packt_AddSlides(PacktPresentation);
   }
// Custom function to add slide with text
   private void Packt_AddSlides(PowerPoint.Presentation
```

```
        PacktPresentationAdd)
{
// Create presentation in powerpoint
    PowerPoint.Presentation PacktPowerPresent = this.Application.
        Presentations.Add(Microsoft.Office.Core.
        MsoTriState.msoTrue);

// Create the custom layout
    PowerPoint.CustomLayout PacktLayout = PacktPowerPresent.
        SlideMaster.CustomLayouts[PowerPoint.PpSlideLayout.
        ppLayoutTitle];

// Add slide to it
    PowerPoint.Slide PacktSlide = PacktPowerPresent.Slides.
        AddSlide(1,PacktLayout);

// Set the title text for the slide
    PacktSlide.Shapes.Title.TextFrame.TextRange.Text = "Book For
        PacktPub";

// Set the text message in the slide
    PacktSlide.Shapes[2].TextFrame.TextRange.Text = "Microsoft
        Office 2007 Programming";
}
```

When you execute this code, you will see a slide and the text, **Book For Packtpub**, as default text, as shown in the following screenshot:

Set the presentation theme

Presentation themes, colors, and properties can be changed using C# programming with the support of VSTO 3.0. Zack has another task at hand—his manager wants all of the PowerPoint applications that have a default white background theme to be changed to some colorful theme. For such a scenario, the `ApplyTheme` method is available in the `PowerPoint.Presentation` object to apply any theme to the entire presentation.

Let's learn how to apply themes using VSTO programming, by examining the following procedure.

Open Visual Studio 2008 and create a new solution, as explained earlier. In the `ThisAddIn.cs` file, write the following program to set a theme for presentation in Microsoft Office PowerPoint 2007:

```
// PowerPoint application object instance
   PowerPoint.Application PacktPowerPointApplication;
   private void ThisAddIn_Startup(object sender, System.EventArgs e)
   {
   // Get access to the instance of current application
      PacktPowerPointApplication = this.Application;
   // Registering the AfterNewPresentation event of the PowerPoint
      PacktPowerPointApplication.AfterNewPresentation +=
         new PowerPoint.EApplication_
         AfterNewPresentationEventHandler(
         PacktPowerPointApplication_AfterNewPresentation);
   }
// AfterNewPresentation event of PowerPoint presentation
   private void PacktPowerPointApplication_AfterNewPresentation(
      PowerPoint.Presentation PacktPresentation)
   {
   // Call the custom function to apply theme
      Packt_ApplyTheme(PacktPresentation);
   }
// Custom function to apply theme
   private void Packt_ApplyTheme(PowerPoint.Presentation
      PacktPresentationAdd)
   {
   // Locating the path where theme files are located in your system
   // .thmx are the theme file format for Microsoft Office PowerPoint
      PacktPresentationAdd.ApplyTheme(@"C:\Program Files\Microsoft
         Office\Document Themes 12\Foundry.thmx");
   }
```

Adding and executing the preceding code, results in a theme as shown in the following screenshot:

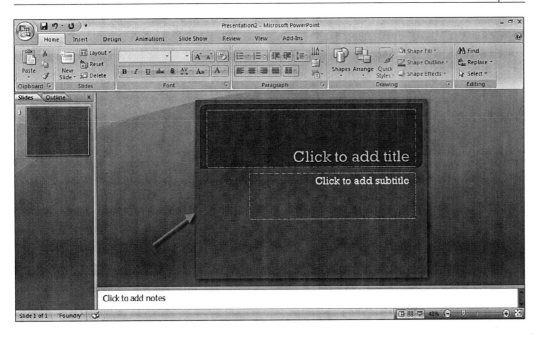

Ribbons in PowerPoint

The Ribbon is the new way of presenting menus for Office 2007 users and organizing related commands. Visually, it appears similar to controls. The Ribbon menu feature is supported in Microsoft Office PowerPoint 2007. Ribbons can be created and customized to fulfil new user requirements.

The previous image illustrates the visual representation of the Ribbon menu in your Microsoft Office PowerPoint 2007 application.

Ribbon Visual Designer

Ribbon Visual Designer is a new option in Visual Studio 2008 that Office developers can use to easily create and customize Ribbons for Office 2007 applications. The features such as drag-and-drop of controls into the Ribbon and easily designing the UI of the Ribbon will give you more productivity by saving more development time.

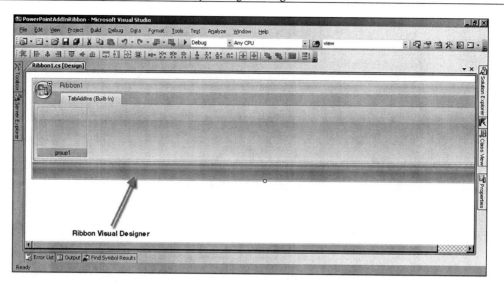

Creating a Ribbon

Let's look at how to create and customize a Ribbon menu for Microsoft Office PowerPoint 2007 using Visual Studio 2008 and VSTO programming. On clicking the button placed in the Ribbon, the custom task pane will be displayed.

1. Open Visual Studio 2008 and create a new solution, as described earlier. To add a Ribbon to your solution, right-click on the project name. From context menu, click on **Add | New Item...**, as shown in the following screenshot:

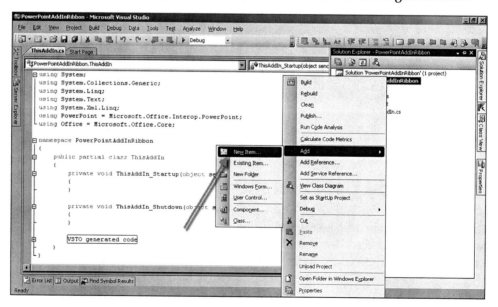

2. Next, select **Ribbon (Visual Designer)** and name the Ribbon **Ribbon1.cs**.

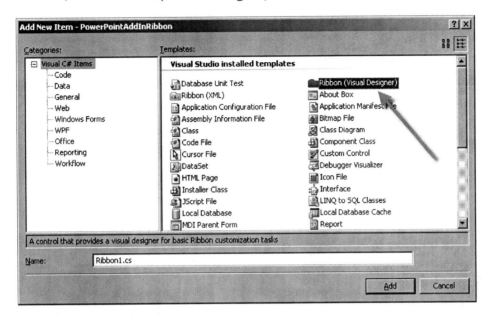

3. On adding the Ribbon to the solution, the Ribbon appears as shown in the following screenshot:

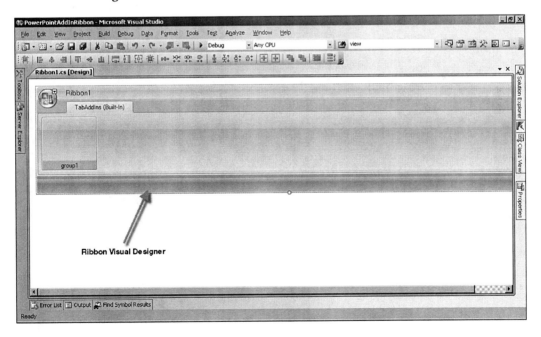

4. Drag-and-drop the control into the Ribbon, as shown in the following screenshot (the button control is added to the Ribbon):

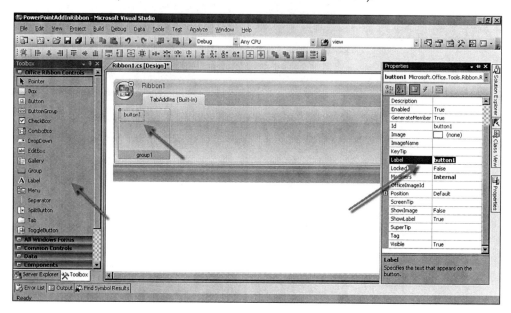

5. Next, you need to add **User Control** to the solution, in order to develop a custom task pane for PowerPoint 2007. Again, right-click on the project name. From the context menu, click on **Add | New Item...**, as shown in the following screenshot:

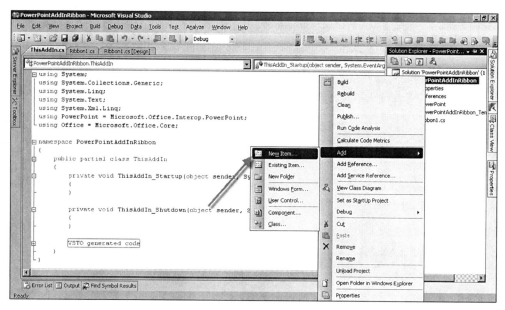

6. Next, select the **User Control**, and name it **UserControl1.cs**.

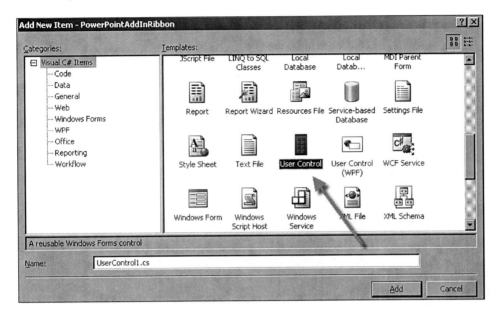

7. Open the **UserControl1.cs** file, and add the following namespace references:

```
using System.Windows.Forms;
using Office = Microsoft.Office.Core;
using PowerPoint = Microsoft.Office.Interop.PowerPoint;
```

8. Open the **Ribbon1.cs** file, and add the following namespace references:

```
using System.Windows.Forms;
using Office = Microsoft.Office.Core;
using PowerPoint = Microsoft.Office.Interop.PowerPoint;
```

9. Next, add the instance of the **User Control** and custom task pane to the Ribbon code file:

```
// Usercontrol instance to access from the Ribbon
    private UserControl1 PacktUserControl;
// Instance for Custom Task Pane to create
    private Microsoft.Office.Tools.CustomTaskPane PacktCustomPane;
```

10. Next, write the following code to show the custom task pane in the button click event of the Ribbon menu:

```
private void RibbonButton1_Click(object sender,
    RibbonControlEventArgs e)
{
// Initializing the UserControl in the ribbon
    PacktUserControl = new UserControl1();

// Add the UserControl to the custom task pane
    PacktCustomPane = Globals.ThisAddIn.CustomTaskPanes.
        Add(PacktUserControl, "Calendar");

// Set the custom task pane to visible
    PacktCustomPane.Visible = true;
}
```

11. On the `ValueChanged` event of the `dateTimePicker`, we are writing the code to insert the selected date.

```
private void dateTimePicker1_ValueChanged(object sender,
    EventArgs e)
{
    try
    {
// Getting the active presentation slide
        PowerPoint.Slide PckTSlide = Globals.ThisAddIn.
            Application.ActivePresentation.Slides[1];
// Set the presentation type like text or image imsert option
        PacktTextShape = PckTSlide.Shapes.AddTextbox(Office.
            MsoTextOrientation.msoTextOrientationHorizontal,
            50, 100, 600, 50);
// Set the text value as selected date time
        PacktTextShape.TextFrame.TextRange.Text = dateTimePicker1.
            Value.ToString();
// Font style properties
        PacktTextShape.TextFrame.TextRange.Font.Size = 48;
        PacktTextShape.TextFrame.TextRange.Font.Color.RGB = Color.
            DarkViolet.ToArgb();
    }
    catch (Exception ex)
    {
        MessageBox.Show(ex.ToString());
    }
}
```

The output of executing this procedure can be seen in the following screenshot:

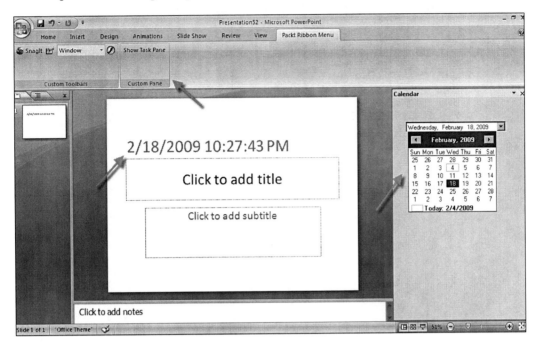

Programming Visio 2007

Microsoft Office Visio is a dominant application for developing sophisticated models. A model is an abstract representation of a system that specifies the modeled system from a firm viewpoint and at a certain level of abstraction. Microsoft Office Visio is the finest design tool for creating shapes, construction diagrams, flow diagrams, database design diagrams, and other design diagrams.

Let's consider a scenario. Zack wants to say hello to all the Visio 2007 users in the office, and Zack is interested in doing this by using VSTO and Visual Studio 2008. The following example demonstrates how Zack implemented this using VSTO programming.

Let's see how to create the solution for Microsoft Office Visio 2007 using Visual
Studio 2008, and write **Hello World** program as your first programming using VSTO
3.0 for Microsoft Visio 2007.

1. Open Visual Studio 2008 to create a new **Visio 2007 Add-in** template project.

2. Select **New Project**. Under **Office** select **2007**, and then select the **Visio 2007
   Add-in** template and name the project as per your requirements.

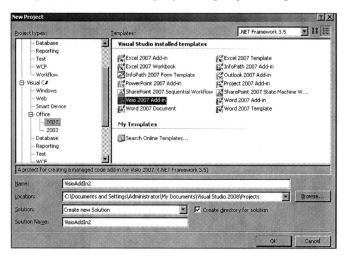

3. The solution will be created with all of supporting files required for the
   development of our Visio solution.

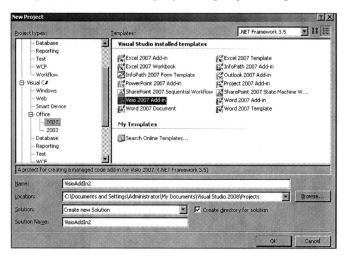

4. In the `ThisAddIn.cs` file, write the following program to say **Hello World** to the Microsoft Office Visio users. Add the `using System.Windows.Forms` namespace for the message box window.

```
private void ThisAddIn_Startup(object sender, System.EventArgs e)
{
// Message box to display information from Visio
    MessageBox.Show("Say Hello World!");
}
```

As it can be seen in the following screenshot, **Say Hello World** is displayed in a message box:

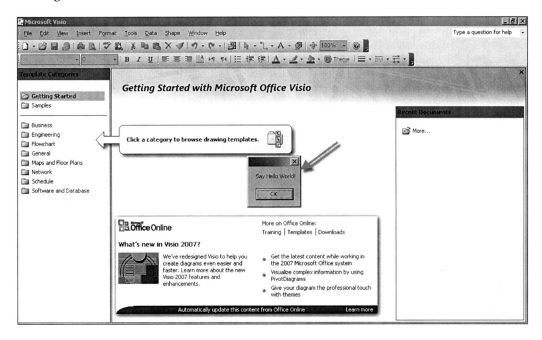

Visio 2007 object model

Visio applications are fully supported by Visual Studio Tools for Office, and work with the objects model by using managed code. Using Visual Studio 2008, you have the full control necessary to develop custom solutions for Visio 2007 with the help of VSTO add-ins and project templates.

By using the object model, you will considerably reduce your development cycle. For example, built-in classes offered by the object model expose methods that will solve many of your requirements, and also save development time.

Dynamically creating a new Visio document

The main advantage of programming for any kind of application is automating some of the manual operations. For any kind of document-based applications, creating a new document will be the primary operation to be performed. To test the ability of programming support for the application, we can create the new document dynamically by using the programming language supported for customizing the application.

Let's create a sample exercise for creating a Visio document dynamically by using VSTO and C# programming.

Open Visual Studio 2008 to create a new Visio solution, as described earlier. Write the following program to create a Visio document dynamically in the ThisAddIn.cs file:

```
private void ThisAddIn_Startup(object sender, System.EventArgs e)
{
// Instance for Document object and calling the Add method on the
   Document collection
   Visio.Document PacktVisioDocument = this.Application.Documents.
      Add("");
// Instance of Shape object
// Page Object has a PageSheet to set other page properties
   Visio.Shape PacktShape = PacktVisioDocument.Pages[1].PageSheet;
// Set the page width property
   PacktShape.get_Cells("PageWidth").Formula = "13.5 in";
// Set the page height property
   PacktShape.get_Cells("PageHeight").Formula = "5.5 in";
}
```

The dynamically-created Visio document, as a result of executing this code, can be seen in the following screenshot:

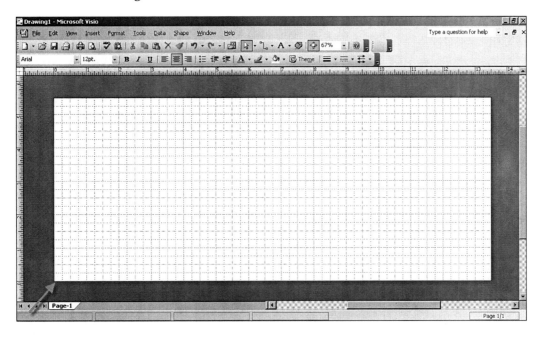

Adding shapes to a document at runtime

Microsoft Office Visio supports drawing shapes in the document. In Visio, shapes represent objects and meaningful concepts. A line, 2-D shapes, or even complex calendars are represented as shapes in the Visio application. Each and every shape has its own behavior corresponding to its drawing type.

Zack is facing a new problem now. He wants to prove the ability of VSTO customization for Visio 2007. His manager is not convinced of VSTO's ability to create shapes, add them to the document, and change their properties at runtime. Zack has to show him the capability of VSTO over Visio 2007. He has created an example to show his manager how to add shapes to the Visio document dynamically.

Let's take a look at the example that Zack created:

Open Visual Studio 2008 to create a new Visio solution, as described earlier. In the `ThisAddIn.cs` file, write the following program, to create a Visio document dynamically:

```
private void ThisAddIn_Startup(object sender, System.EventArgs e)
{
// Instance for Document object and calling the Add method on
    the Document collection
    Visio.Document PacktVisioDocument = this.Application.
        Documents.Add("");
// Instance of Shape object
// Page Object has a PageSheet to set other page properties
    Visio.Shape PacktShape = PacktVisioDocument.Pages[1].PageSheet;
// Set the page width property
    PacktShape.get_Cells("PageWidth").Formula = "5.5 in";
// Set the page height property
    PacktShape.get_Cells("PageHeight").Formula = "2.5 in";
// Code to add Shape to the document
// Access the Shapes file through Document object
    Visio.Document PacktDocStencil = Application.Documents.
        OpenEx("BASIC_M.VSS", (short)Visio.VisOpenSaveArgs.
        visOpenDocked);
// Drop the new Square Shape to our Visio document
    Visio.Shape PacktShape2 = PacktShape.Drop(PacktDocStencil.
        Masters["Square"], 10, 7.50);
// Adding text to inside the Shape
    PacktShape2.Text = "Packt Shape One";
}
```

The dynamically-created square shape, with the text **Packt Shape One**, will be created, as shown in the following screenshot:

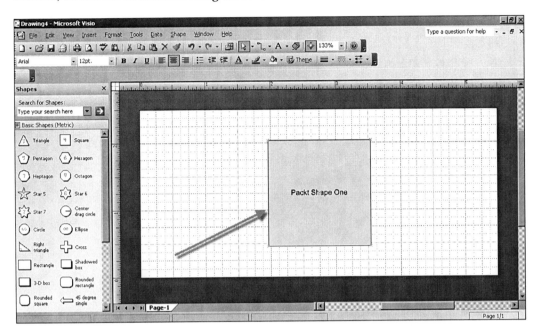

Adding a page as a background for another page

Let's see how to use a page as a background for another page. In this example, a document will contain two pages—the first page will be the work space that holds all of the shapes and objects, while the other page will act as the background image for the first page.

Open Visual Studio 2008 to create a new Visio solution, as explained earlier. In the ThisAddIn.cs file, write the following program to create a Visio document dynamically:

```
private void ThisAddIn_Startup(object sender, System.EventArgs e)
{
// Instance for Document object and calling the Add method on
    the Document collection
    Visio.Document PacktVisioDocument = this.Application.
        Documents.Add("");
// Instance of Shape object
// Page Object has a PageSheet to set other page properties
    Visio.Shape PacktShape = PacktVisioDocument.Pages[1].PageSheet;
// Set the page width property
    PacktShape.get_Cells("PageWidth").Formula = "6 in";
```

```
    // Set the page height property
        PacktShape.get_Cells("PageHeight").Formula = "3 in";
    // Adding the page for background
        Visio.Page PacktBgPage = Application.ActiveDocument.Pages.Add();
    // Set the name for new page
        PacktBgPage.Name = "Packt Page BackGround";
    //Set the  background code property
        PacktBgPage.Background = 3;
    // The new page will be the backgroud for the current page
        Application.ActiveDocument.Pages[1].BackPage = PacktBgPage.Name;
    // New shape instance
        Visio.Shape PacktTextShape = null;
    // Read the page of the current document
        PacktTextShape = PacktVisioDocument.Pages[2].PageSheet;
    // Create rectangle
        PacktTextShape.DrawRectangle(1.0, 10.0, 3.0, 10.5);
    // Set the text style
        PacktTextShape.TextStyle = "Normal";
    // Set the line style
        PacktTextShape.LineStyle = "Text Only";
    // New instance of Character object
        Visio.Characters PacktText = null;
    // Assign the characters of the shape to the Visio character object
        PacktText = Application.ActiveDocument.Pages[2].Shapes.
            get_ItemFromID(PacktTextShape.ID+1).Characters;
    // Set the begin point
        PacktText.Begin = 0;
    // Set the end point
        PacktText.End = 25;
    // Text for the rectangle
        PacktText.Text = "My First BOOK";
    }
```

The page that is acting as the background page has a rectangular shape that contains the text, **My First BOOK** on it. You can see the following screenshot when you click the **Page-1** tab:

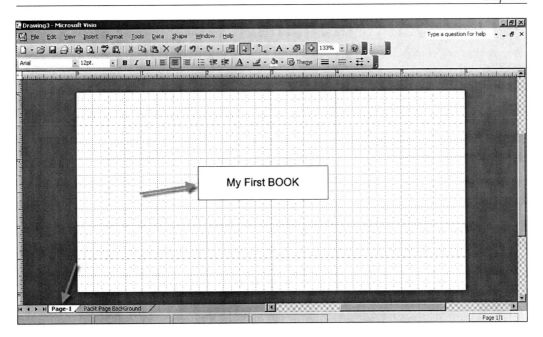

When you click the **Packt Page BackGround** tab, you can see the following screenshot:

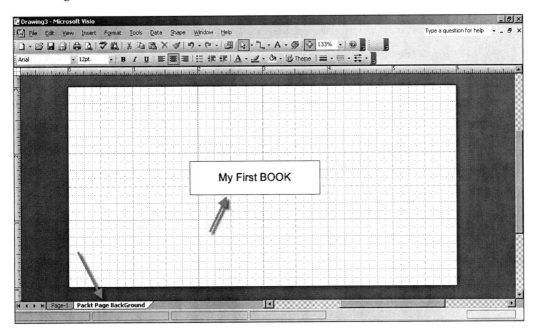

Set the document theme

The objects available in the VSTO object model can be used to change the theme of the Visio document. `ThemeColors` is the object used to manage the themes for Visio documents. Under the `ActivePage` object, the `ThemeColors` and `ThemeEffects` property is exposed when accessed through the `Application` object. The colors available in the `Visio.VisThemeColors` object are assigned to the `ThemeColors`. Similarly, the themes available for the `Visio.VisThemeEffects` object are assigned to the `ThemeEffects`.

Let's see an example of how to change the default theme for shapes inside the document, and give new color themes, programmatically, by using VSTO and C#.

Open Visual Studio 2008 to create a new Visio solution, as described earlier. In the `ThisAddIn.cs` file, write the following program to set the theme for a Visio document:

```csharp
private void ThisAddIn_S tartup(object sender, System.EventArgs e)
{
// Instance for Document object and calling the Add method on
    the Document collection
    Visio.Document PacktVisioDocument = this.Application.
        Documents.Add("");
// Instance of Shape object
// Page Object has a PageSheet to set other page properties
    Visio.Shape PacktShape = PacktVisioDocument.Pages[1].PageSheet;
// Set the page width property
    PacktShape.get_Cells("PageWidth").Formula = "6 in";
// Set the page height property
    PacktShape.get_Cells("PageHeight").Formula = "3 in";
// Code to add Shape to the document
// Access the Shapes file through Document object
    Visio.Document PacktDocStencil = Application.Documents.
        OpenEx("BASIC_M.VSS", (short)Visio.VisOpenSaveArgs.
        visOpenDocked);
// Drop the new Square Shape to our Visio document
    Visio.Shape PacktShape1 = PacktShape.
        Drop(PacktDocStencil.Masters["Circle"], 2, 2);
// Adding text to inside the Shape
    PacktShape1.Text = "Packt Shape One";
// Drop the new Triangle Shape to our Visio document
    Visio.Shape PacktShape2 = PacktShape.
        Drop(PacktDocStencil.Masters["Triangle"], 3, 3);
// Adding text to inside the Shape
```

```
        PacktShape2.Text = "Packt Shape Two";
    // Set the theme color for the Shapes in the active page
        Application.ActivePage.ThemeColors = Visio.VisThemeColors.
            visThemeColorsMedianDark;
    // Set the theme effect for the Shapes in the active page
        Application.ActivePage.ThemeEffects = Visio.
            VisThemeEffects.visThemeEffectsMesh;
    }
```

On executing this code, you get the following output:

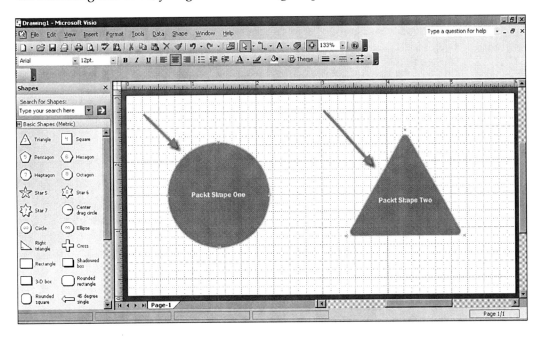

Creating a Commandbar

The **Commandbar** is the main control panel for most of the functions available in the application. The Commandbar is easily accessible and is visible near the top of the applications screen. VSTO objects help you to customize your existing Commandbar, or build your own custom Commandbar, for Visio 2007.

In this example, you are going to learn how to create a new custom Commandbar and add a button to it, enabling a click event for the button.

Open Visual Studio 2008 to create a new Visio solution, as explained earlier. Write the following code to create a Commandbar for Visio in the `ThisAddIn.cs` file.

```csharp
// Namespace to access Windows Form features
   using System.Windows.Forms;
// Instance of the CommandBars collection object
   private Office.CommandBars PacktCommandBarCollection;
// Instance of the CommandBar object
   private Office.CommandBar PacktCommandBar;
// Instance of CommandBarButton control
   private Office.CommandBarButton PacktBookList;

   private void ThisAddIn_Startup(object sender, System.EventArgs e)
   {
// Access the current application's CommandBars
      PacktCommandBarCollection = (Office.CommandBars)this.
         Application.CommandBars;
// Add the new CommandBar to the CommandBar list with name, type,
   and so on.
      PacktCommandBar = PacktCommandBarCollection.Add(
         "PacktVisioBar", Office.MsoBarPosition.msoBarTop,
         Type.Missing, true);
// Add the CommandBarButton to your new CommandBar
      PacktBookList = (Office.CommandBarButton)PacktCommandBar.
         Controls.Add(Office.MsoControlType.msoControlButton, 1,
         Type.Missing,1, true);
// Set tag property to the CommandButton
      PacktBookList.Tag = "Packt Book List";

// Set the tooltip property of the CommandButton
      PacktBookList.TooltipText = "Made for Packt";

// Register the click event for the button
      PacktBookList.Click += new Office.
         _CommandBarButtonEvents_ClickEventHandler(
         PacktBookList_Click);
   }
// Click event of the CommandButton control
   private void PacktBookList_Click(Office.CommandBarButton Ctrl,
      ref bool CancelDefault)
   {
// Message to button clicked users
      MessageBox.Show("books are in progress...");
   }
```

The CommandBar that we created by adding the preceding code can be seen in the following screenshot:

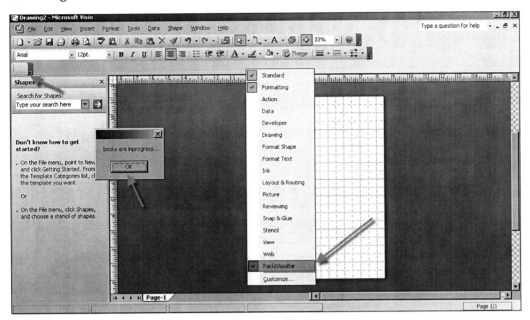

Programming Project 2007

Microsoft Office Project is a specialized project management application that stores and manages a large volume of data related to your project. This, data can include the project name, description, tasks and durations, project resource names, calendars, assignments, costs, milestones, and more. Project managers use Microsoft Office Project to enter, save, and update project information. They can then send updated project information such as assignments or task updates to specific resources.

Microsoft Office Project 2007 provides you with excellent project management features, through easy-to-use management tools and flexible working tools. By using Microsoft Office Project 2007, project management is made simpler for project managers. Managers can track and examine projects effectively with an enhanced view of the schedule and the supporting functionality to manage it.

VSTO provides application-level solution development and customization for Microsoft Office Project 2007. You can create application-level add-ins for Microsoft Office Project 2007 using Visual Studio 2008.

1. Open Visual Studio 2008, to create a new **Project 2007 Add-in** template project.
2. Select **New Project**. Under **Office** select **2007**, and then choose the **Project Add-in** template and name the project as per your requirements.

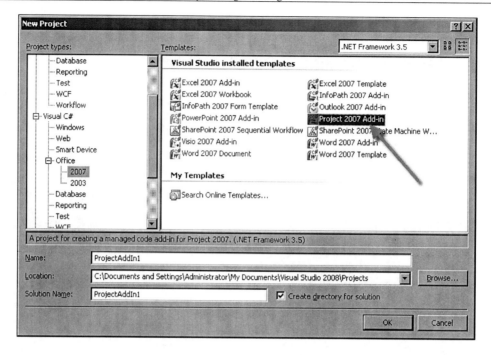

3. The solution will be created with all the supporting files needed for the development of our Project solution, as shown in the **Solution Explorer**:

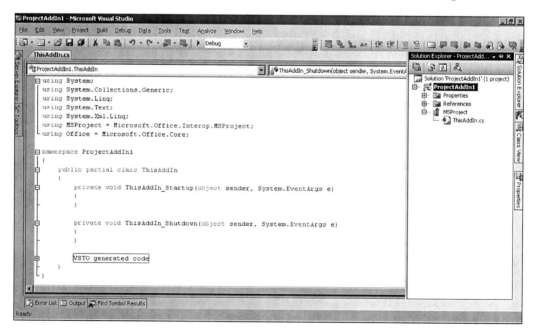

4. In the `ThisAddIn.cs` file, write the following program to say **Say! Hello World** to all Microsoft Project users:

```
// Namespace to access Windows Form features
using System.Windows.Forms;

private void ThisAddIn_Startup(object sender, System.EventArgs e)
{
// Message displayed to all Project 2007 users
    MessageBox.Show("Say! Hello World");
}
```

On executing this code, a message box containing the text **Say! Hello World** is displayed in Microsoft Project, as shown in the following screenshot:

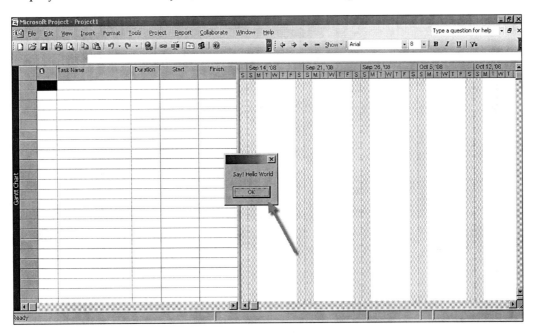

Creating a Project and adding a task dynamically

`MSProject.Project` is the main object used for Microsoft Project programming using VSTO. The `MSProject.Project` object exposes several project-related properties, such as the `Name` property that sets the name of the project, and the `Manager` property that assigns the manager name for the project.

Let's see an example of how to create a new project and add a task item to it, by using the VSTO objects available for Microsoft Project.

Open Visual Studio 2008, to create a new Project solution, as described earlier. Write the following code in the `ThisAddIn.cs` file:

```
private void ThisAddIn_Startup(object sender, System.EventArgs e)
{
// Using project object to create new project document
    MSProject.Project PacktProject = Application.Projects.Add(false,
        Type.Missing, false);

// Set the Name for project
    PacktProject.Name = "New Book for Packt";

// Add the project manager
    PacktProject.Manager = "Radhika";

// Get the active project
    PacktProject = Globals.ThisAddIn.Application.ActiveProject;

// Add the task to the active project
    PacktProject.Tasks.Add("Prepare Topic", Type.Missing);

}
```

The results of executing this code can be seen in the following screenshot:

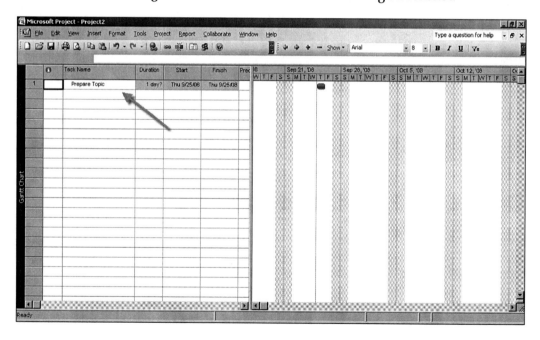

Creating menus for Microsoft Project

Microsoft Office Project 2007 provides a very good visual representation of menus for user interaction with the application. Microsoft Project provides support for menu customization in order to improve customized visual interaction with users. VSTO 3.0 offers extensive options to build custom menus and to customize existing menus to suit users' needs.

Let's see an example of how to create a menu for Microsoft Project by using VSTO objects.

Open Visual Studio 2008, to create a new Project solution, as done earlier. Write the following code in the `ThisAddIn.cs` file.

```csharp
// The menu details at class level.
    private Office.CommandBarButton PacktMenuCmd;

    private void ThisAddIn_Startup(object sender, System.EventArgs e)
    {
    // Initialize the CommandBarPopup object
        Office.CommandBarPopup PacktCmdBarCtrl = null;

    // Get the active menubar in the application
        Office.CommandBar PacktMenuBar = (Office.
            CommandBar)Application.CommandBars.ActiveMenuBar;

    // Get the total controls count in menubar
        int ctrlCount = PacktMenuBar.Controls.Count;

    // Add the menu with control in the application interface
        PacktCmdBarCtrl = (Office.CommandBarPopup)PacktMenuBar.
            Controls.Add(Office.MsoControlType.msoControlPopup,
            missing, missing, ctrlCount, true);

    // Check for commandbar
        if (PacktCmdBarCtrl != null)
        {
        // Set the caption property of the commandbar
            PacktCmdBarCtrl.Caption = "Packt Book Project";

        // Set the Tag property of the commandbar
            PacktCmdBarCtrl.Tag = "Tag to identify our Menu";

        // Adding the menu command to the commandbar
            PacktMenuCmd = (Office.CommandBarButton)PacktCmdBarCtrl.
                Controls.Add(Office.MsoControlType.msoControlButton,
                missing, missing, missing, true);
```

```
            PacktMenuCmd.Caption = "Pack Microsoft Books";
            PacktMenuCmd.Tag = "Tag Microsoft Books";
            PacktMenuCmd.FaceId = 61;
        // Click event handler for the menu item
            PacktMenuCmd.Click += new Microsoft.Office.Core.
                _CommandBarButtonEvents_ClickEventHandler(
                menuCommand_Click);

        }
    }
    // Add text to cell A1 when the menu is clicked.
        private void menuCommand_Click(Microsoft.Office.Core.
            CommandBarButton Ctrl, ref bool CancelDefault)
        {
            MessageBox.Show("Packt Menu Clicked");
        }
```

The results of executing the code can be seen in the following screenshot:

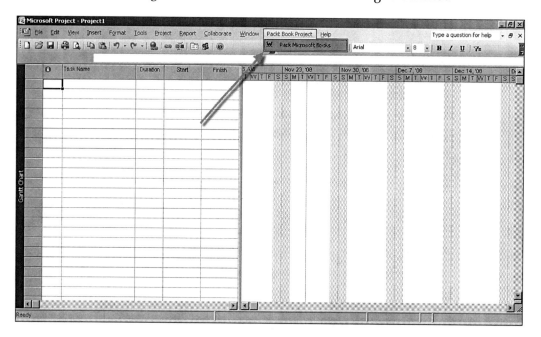

Creating a Commandbar for Microsoft Project

Most user interfaces for applications have a Commandbar that has buttons, menus, and input or output control elements for user interaction with the application. `Office.CommandBar` is an object in VSTO that is used to create the Commandbar menu in the Microsoft Office 2007 application.

Let's see an example of how to create a Commandbar menu for Microsoft Project by using VSTO objects.

Open Visual Studio 2008, to create a new Project solution. Write the following code in the `ThisAddIn.cs` file:

```
// Office commandbar initializing
    Office.CommandBar PacktCmdBar;
// Office commandbarbutton initializing
    Office.CommandBarButton PacktButton;

    private void ThisAddIn_Startup(object sender, System.EventArgs e)
    {
    // Commandbar object indexing
        if (PacktCmdBar == null)
        {
        // Add a commandbar named 'Export Data'
            PacktCmdBar = Application.CommandBars.Add("Export Data",
                1, missing, true);
        }
    // Adding button to the commandbar and event handler.
        PacktButton = (Office.CommandBarButton)PacktCmdBar.Controls.
            Add(1, missing, missing, missing, missing);
    // Set the button style property
        PacktButton.Style = Office.MsoButtonStyle.
            msoButtonIconAndCaption;
    // Set the caption for the Button
        PacktButton.Caption = "Export Data";
    // Set the tag for the Button
        PacktButton.Tag = "Export Data Tag";
    // Click event for the Button in the commandbar
        PacktButton.Click += new Office.
            _CommandBarButtonEvents_ClickEventHandler(ButtonClick);
    // Set the commandbar to visible
        PacktCmdBar.Visible = true;
    }
// Click event for the button in the commandbar
    private void ButtonClick(Office.CommandBarButton PacktCtrl,
        ref bool cancel)
    {
    // Message to be displayed
        MessageBox.Show("Set your operation here!");
    }
```

The result of executing this code can be seen in the following screenshot:

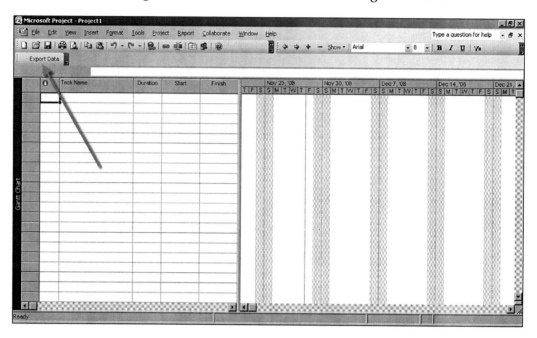

Summary

In this chapter, you have learned the concept of programming with PowerPoint 2007 using VSTO 3.0. You learned about the object models of PowerPoint and worked out sample solutions. You learned how to create a presentation, how to add slides, and how to format the text inside the slides using VSTO and C# programming. You learned the concept of the Ribbon menu in the PowerPoint application, and how to create and customize a Ribbon. In the second half of this chapter, you learned about programming for Visio 2007. You learned the concept of programming in Visio 2007 using VSTO 3.0. You have also learned the object models of Visio and worked on some examples. You learned how to create and manage shapes in Visio by using VSTO and C# programming. You have also learned programming in Project 2007 using VSTO 3.0.

Index

Thank you for buying
VSTO 3.0 for Office 2007 Programming

About Packt Publishing

Packt, pronounced 'packed', published its first book "*Mastering phpMyAdmin for Effective MySQL Management*" in April 2004 and subsequently continued to specialize in publishing highly focused books on specific technologies and solutions.

Our books and publications share the experiences of your fellow IT professionals in adapting and customizing today's systems, applications, and frameworks. Our solution based books give you the knowledge and power to customize the software and technologies you're using to get the job done. Packt books are more specific and less general than the IT books you have seen in the past. Our unique business model allows us to bring you more focused information, giving you more of what you need to know, and less of what you don't.

Packt is a modern, yet unique publishing company, which focuses on producing quality, cutting-edge books for communities of developers, administrators, and newbies alike. For more information, please visit our website: www.packtpub.com.

Writing for Packt

We welcome all inquiries from people who are interested in authoring. Book proposals should be sent to author@packtpub.com. If your book idea is still at an early stage and you would like to discuss it first before writing a formal book proposal, contact us; one of our commissioning editors will get in touch with you.

We're not just looking for published authors; if you have strong technical skills but no writing experience, our experienced editors can help you develop a writing career, or simply get some additional reward for your expertise.

Microsoft Visual C++ Windows Applications by Example

ISBN: 978-1-847195-56-2   Paperback: 440 pages

Code and explanation for real-world MFC C++ Applications

1. Learn C++ Windows programming by studying realistic, interesting examples

2. A quick primer in Visual C++ for programmers of other languages, followed by deep, thorough examples

3. Example applications include a Tetris-style game, a spreadsheet application, a drawing application, and a word processor

4. Each application demonstrates key real-world techniques: parsing text, working with files, creating memory structures, displaying interactive graphics, and more

Software Testing with Visual Studio Team System 2008

ISBN: 978-1-847195-58-6   Paperback: 340 pages

A comprehensive and concise guide to testing your software applications with Visual Studio Team System 2008

1. Test your software applications with Visual Studio Team System 2008 and rest assured of its quality

2. Create a structured testing environment for your applications to produce reliable products

3. Comprehensive yet concise guide with a lot of examples and clear explanations

Please check **www.PacktPub.com** for information on our titles

Printed in the United States
141051LV00003B/20/P